THE
TRANSFORMING
POWER
OF THE
BIBLE

THE
TRANSFORMING
POWER
OF THE
BIBLE

Wayne Bradley Robinson

THE PILGRIM PRESS
NEW YORK

Library of Congress Cataloging in Publication Data

Robinson, Wayne Bradley, 1936–
   The transforming power of the Bible.

   Includes bibliograhical references.
   1. Bible—Study. I. Title.
BS600.2.R63   1984   220'.07   83-23680
ISBN 0-8298-0706-3 (pbk.)

The Pilgrim Press, 132 West 31 Street, New York, NY 10001

CONTENTS

ACKNOWLEDGMENTS

I express my appreciation to the many people who have participated in the groups I have led through the method of using scripture described in this book. I have benefited greatly from their responses to questions and from their evaluations of the method. I especially acknowledge the following persons: Charles Melchert, my dialogue partner during the initial phase of developing my method of working with scripture; Donald Sevetson, the first person to challenge me to start teaching my method to others; Walter Wink and Frank Pirazzini, whose encouragement led to the writing of this book; Sharon Ringe and Victor Hallberg (and Walter Wink), whose feedback on the manuscript was so helpful; Mary Ann Mead, who helped me rework the diagrams in Chapters III and IV and prepared the final drawings; Carol Tollin and Carol Rud, who translated my handwriting into a typed manuscript; the members of the First Congregational Church of Robbinsdale (UCC), for granting me sabbatical time to complete this book; and my wife, Hannelore, and my children, Paul and Katharine, who have been so much a part of the whole process.

THE
TRANSFORMING
POWER
OF THE
BIBLE

PROLOGUE

In this prologue, I want to share with you something of my personal odyssey with the Bible. My purpose for doing this is twofold. I imagine many of you will find points of identification that may stimulate personal reflection. I also want to be up-front about the roots of the tree that forms the main body of this book.

As I look back I realize that these roots began forming during my sophomore year of high school. Some friends persuaded me to attend a summer conference sponsored by the New York Conference of the Congregational Church. Up to that time I had had little contact with the church and even less contact with the Bible. In fact, the most convincing argument my friends put forth regarding my going to the conference had to do with the members of the opposite sex I would meet if I went.

Once I got there my initial expectations gave way to something more. I was impressed by the caring staff and the loving community created in that time. I found myself caught up in the worship life of the community. I became enthused* about God and what God might want me to do with my life. It was a kind of conversion experience for me. And at the core of it all was the Bible. I began to read it; I wanted to find out how it could continue enriching my life as it had begun to do at that conference. When I returned home I gradually became more active in the local Congregational church and came to believe that God

---

*The word enthused comes from the Greek en *theos*, meaning "in God."

3

was calling me to the ministry and to a special task with regard to the Bible. But both these things remained tentative.

During my college years I became convinced about the ministry part—that was indeed what I wanted to do, and I had a deepening sense of being called into the ministry—but the Bible part was less clear. In my religion courses I learned a lot about the Bible, but that knowledge was not doing for me what I had hoped. The life-giving Spirit of the Bible, to which I had responded earlier in the context of a lively Christian community, seemed to be deadened rather than enhanced by the approach to the Bible presented in those courses. So I deferred my hopes to seminary. When I got there the scriptures would come alive, I thought.

At seminary many things stimulated me on my spiritual journey, but I was discouraged about my courses in Bible, especially those in New Testament—the ones for which I had had the highest hopes. I respected my professors and still feel indebted to them for what they taught me. But all the information I had accumulated did not make the New Testament come alive for me in a way that was personally enriching. Even as I graduated, I felt unprepared to help others use the scriptures in a life-enhancing way. I decided that I needed more information about the New Testament and resolved to go on to obtain a Ph.D. in that field. Perhaps then, I thought, I could reach the point where the New Testament would be what I had hoped. Maybe I just needed to know more.

After seven years of college and seminary, however, I needed a sabbatical from studying and deferred further academic work for a year. After graduation and ordination, I accepted a call to a one-year appointment as associate chaplain at Technical University, in Aachen, Germany. There I found at last something of what I had been searching for. My German colleague Heinz Knorr had brought into being a unique community of students, at the core of which was the New Testament. Every Monday evening we would gather twenty or thirty students to wrestle with the New Testament text for the week. During these Monday evening sessions, Chaplain Knorr or I would read the text and provide some basic historical-critical background for it. The next two hours would be spent in free-flowing discussion. The students would bring their questions, insights, and life experiences to the text and speak to what the text elicited in them. In a sense we came together to read the text, and each time we seemed to emerge with the text having "read" us! Out of the session my colleague or I would prepare a sermon for the Wednesday evening worship service. At the following Monday evening session, we would receive feedback from the students and then move on to the text for the week ahead.

This experience left an indelible impression on me. Most of the students had been turned off by the church and were drawn into this Christian community by the Monday evening sessions. Through these scripture-based sessions, they started taking their faith journeys seriously. The gap I had felt between the academic study of scripture and the life of faith was beginning to close. My hope was renewed. I was now convinced that there was a way to honor the insights and knowledge developed over the centuries in the academic world as well as the insights and experiences of people. I had found the beginnings of the model that I had been searching for. I left Aachen certain about the validity of using the scriptures with a group of people whose expertise was not in the Bible as such but in life itself. I still had many unanswered questions: How and why did New Testament research start? How did it develop? Why did it develop such an impressive body of knowledge but end up so seemingly sterile? What was the relationship between the

Jesus we can get back to by way of historical research and the "Christ" of faith?

I took all these questions with me into my doctoral work at the University of St. Andrews, in Scotland. In pursuing them, I went back to the beginnings of New Testament research and traced its development up to the present. I was especially interested in such New Testament theologians as Günther Bornkamn, Ernst Käsemann, Hans Conzelmann, and Ernst Fuchs, who were wrestling with the renewed interest in the "historical Jesus." When my doctoral work was finished I was both satisfied and frustrated—satisfied that I had gotten one more piece of the puzzle in place and frustrated because I was certain there was more ahead.

What that "more" was became apparent almost immediately when I returned to the United States and went into the parish ministry. By now I knew a lot about the New Testament—especially the Synoptic Gospels*—but I discovered that I knew little about human beings as they existed outside the student world in which I had been immersed for so long. New and urgent questions emerged out of my work with people "out in the world." How do adults change (repent)? What facilitates change, and what inhibits it? How does knowledge—any knowledge, biblical or otherwise—fit into the process? For example, countless smokers know about the detrimental effects of cigarette smoking, but they do not change; they continue to smoke. What does that say about other facts—biblical facts included? What about the relationship between emotions, thoughts, and will? Why had biblical scholars been in conversation with and used the insights of certain philosophers and historians but not conversed with and

---

*Synoptic refers to the Gospels of Mark, Luke, and Matthew, which can be seen together (that is what synoptic means). This is discussed later in more detail.

used the insights of other philosophers or of sociologists and behavioral scientists?

During the next ten years, I spent at least a month of concentrated study and part of almost every week working on deepening my understanding of how we human beings and our social systems function; this was in addition to my work with scripture. I am particularly grateful to the Sealantic Foundation for the fellowship they granted me to explore the behavioral sciences in the initial phase of this project. This support gave me the encouragement I needed to move ahead. Finally, in the late 1970s, the basic system I had been working toward was in place; it combined the basic insights I had drawn from the social and behavioral sciences and the insights of historical-critical work in the New Testament. Since then I have refined the system and field-tested it with various groups—adult laypeople, teenagers, and clergy; their feedback has been exceedingly beneficial to me. I have been deeply moved at the responses of both laypeople and clergy who have found in this approach to scripture something they have been longing for. Once a retired minister came to me at the end of a session with tears in his eyes, saying, "I am so grateful for this new approach because the Bible has become personally meaningful to me for the first time since I was young." It was not just that his response was so touching but that his response was similar to that of many others. During the refining process I have gained knowledge from two of my colleagues and friends, Walter Wink and Sharon Ringe, and from members of the Guild for Psychological Studies.

The pilgrimage has been long—much longer than I realized until I started writing this prologue. In the process, I moved from initial enthusiasm to discouragement to wistful longing. And I am now finally confident about the possibility of using scripture in a way that helps people move toward wholeness, that has intellectual integrity and affective (emotional) impact, and that truly facilitates change. Each time I lead a group in this method of using scripture I do so in the expectation that indeed "God hath yet more light and truth to break forth from the Holy Word."[1] I've seen it happen again and again. I know it works. A couple of summers ago, while leading a group of adults in the sequence on "Like a Child," some people came to me halfway through and said, "Could you tone this scripture stuff down a bit—it's really getting to us." In liberal circles that is a rare (and welcome) complaint.

The first chapters deal with some of the background, which will help those who would like to lead others in using the method I've developed. This background material will also be useful to anyone who is interested in a fresh approach to scripture but is not necessarily planning to become a leader. There is also a section on specifics, which explains the various parts of the method, as well as a detailed description of the method itself. The final four chapters present four sequences that are how-to samples of the method at work.

When dealing with new material, I read the introduction, scan the middle, and read the conclusion. Then I go back and read from beginning to end. This method helps me absorb more of what is being said. This technique may also be helpful to you. To aid you in the process, I have summarized below the seven steps in the "moving toward wholeness" method. These steps are amplified and explained in the opening chapters.

Step 1. Active Listening

Active listening involves getting inside the text on its own terms. It is similar to what a therapist does in order to respond to a counselee. In counseling, this involves a suspension of judgment and a disciplined effort to get inside the counselee's world as the counselee sees and understands it. Among the therapist's principal tools for doing this are questions that emerge out of active listening and that help the therapist and the counselee understand the many dimensions of the issues in the counselee's life. In the method I have developed, something similar is done with the text. The text is set, as it were, in the center of a group of twelve to twenty people. The leader's task is to share questions that emerge from the text and that have been prepared in advance. The group's task is to come up with as many "hunches"* as possible in response to the questions.

Step 2. Bridge-building

Bridge-building also has some similarity to the counseling process. Often after a counseling session I think about what the other person has said and realize that his or her story is my story too—that I have been in a place like the place he or she is in, even though I was not clear about that previously. The first part of this step in responding to a text involves intentionally engaging in this kind of activity. The leader invites the members of the group to do something that has been designed in advance and seems appropriate to the specific text, something that will become a bridge across which the person(s) or pieces of the text can walk to call forth the "twin" in each of us. The second part involves sharing verbally what each of us has found out about himself or herself, so that a second

---

*Throughout this book I use the word hunch in a special way. The word guess suggests something random, something to which one has not given much thought. The word answer suggests something of which only one can be right. I chose the word hunch because it conveys, for me, the sense of using one's intuition, one's creative imagination, one's capacity for insight. A hunch comes from looking at what one sees and hears and going beyond to the truths that that sensory data both convey and veil.

"bridge" can be crossed—this time from our inner selves to the world outside.

Step 3. Identifying Learnings

From the first two steps people almost always learn or relearn something about themselves, and it is important to get that down in writing so it can be utilized in the succeeding steps. For Step 3, each person is invited to write down what she or he has learned about or for herself or himself out of Step 1 and Step 2 (not what the text "means" in the abstract).

Step 4. Identifying Wants

Identifying wants involves challenging people to identify and write down what they want to do about what they have learned about or for themselves (not what they "should" or "ought to" do).

Step 5. Goal-setting

Using the guidelines for goal-setting that are presented later, people are invited to transform their "want" statements into short-term behavioral goals.

Step 6. Covenanting

After completing Step 5, people are asked to pair off and to refine their goals so that they fit the guidelines. Then each person is asked to state his or her goal to the others, make a commitment to carry out that goal, and set a procedure for sharing with others how it went.

Step 7. Sharing How It Went

This step simply involves doing what was agreed to in the last part of Step 6.

When presenting this method to groups, I am often asked whether it works with all kinds of texts. In my experience it can, but it is most easily applied to narrative material, where people are saying and doing things. Initially, I developed the method with the Synoptic Gospels in mind and then expanded it for use with other texts. It is more difficult to use with material like Paul's letters. I do not want to claim that this is the only valid way to use scripture, but I am convinced that this method effectively facilitates healing changes in people's lives, and that is the major reason I want to share it with others through this book.

Also I have been asked how my work relates to that of Walter Wink. This book provides the most effective answer to that question. What Walter Wink and I share above all is a common commitment to releasing scripture as an agent of human transformation. The principal contribution that he and members of the Guild for Psychological Studies have made to my work is to deepen my understanding of the use of questions in Step 1. The most significant difference is in Steps 3 to 7, which are unique to my work.

Another common question relates to the significance of my title for the method—Moving Toward Wholeness. It points to what I have seen happen in people's lives when working with scripture in the way outlined above. For me, the word wholeness signifies that toward which or away from which I see life constantly moving. The word whole goes back to the Old English word *hal*, from which we get the word healthy. It is related to the German word *Heil*, which means both "health" and "salvation." My basic assumptions related to the idea of wholeness are (1) that we are born with a kind of basic nascent wholeness (original goodness); (2) that as we grow up we are always moving both away from and toward a wholeness that will always be "out there," beyond our grasp; (3) that part of our movement away from wholeness happens when we lose or suppress pieces of ourselves that we need to become more whole; and (4) that recovery of these lost pieces is crucial to our becoming both more whole *again, and* more whole than we ever were before. The scriptures can be or become again a powerful aid in recovering and reintegrating the lost pieces of ourselves, empowering us to move toward wholeness.

CHAPTER I

The Living Authority of Scripture

The Dynamics of Authority

"They were all dumbfounded and began to ask one another, 'What is this? A new kind of teaching! He speaks with authority' . . . unlike the doctors of the law [Mark 1:27, 22, NEB]." What was so new about Jesus' teaching? Does it still hit us in a "new" way? If not, why not? How did his "authority" differ from that of the scribes, or doctors of the law? Who are these scribes anyway? Maybe they hold a clue. Although often maligned in the New Testament, the scribes were respected people. They were the ones who really knew scripture. They were the experts, the scholars. In many ways they were the first-century counterparts of today's biblical scholars. The similarities are striking. Matthew Black says of the scribes:

They were men of sacred letters, occupying themselves in gathering together Israel's sacred literature as well as interpreting it; in addition they were copyists, editors, and guardians of the textual purity of scripture. . . . It was to their faithful transmission of the religion of Israel in the Greek and Roman periods that we owe the preservation of Old Testament scriptures, together with the foundations in Judaism of the Christian religion.[1]

Generally, then, the scribal teacher-scholars were much like the academic teacher-scholars of our time. There is certainly value in this approach. Historical-critical work, like scribal work, does help to preserve the "purity of the text." Historical-critical work also guards against misuse of the Bible and preserves its otherness and strangeness. It is also the best tool for unearthing the needed background for understanding a given biblical passage. But like the work of the scribes, it is not enough. If it shares the strength of the scribal approach, it also shares its weakness. It lacks the authority that makes things happen in people's lives. With its emphasis on the rational and the critical, it can actually contribute to taming the impact scripture can have.

Jesus' teaching did not fit this model. It is important to pay attention not only to what Jesus taught but also to how he taught. To be sure, he did use some contemporary teaching forms, such as parables, and he had a thorough knowledge of the scriptures, as did the scribes. But his teaching arose out of a different dimension of himself. *Exousia* (authority) literally means "out of (one's) being"; Jesus' teaching arose out of the depths of his being and touched people in the deepest places of themselves. It focused on the here and now and on a person-to-person encounter that included *all* dimensions of human life. This is why it had a dramatic impact on the lives of those touched by it. To the scribal kind of teaching one could respond, "I understand what you are saying, and that is interesting. However. . . ." But when Jesus taught, people were amazed; they were moved; their lives were transformed; they were healed. They also resisted him mightily, claiming, as his family did, that he was crazy (literally "beside himself [Mark 3:21]"). Or, like some of the scribes, they believed his power was demonic (Mark 3:22). One reaction was excluded—detached neutrality. As Rudolf Bultmann rightly says, Jesus put people in the position of either/or. Jesus' teaching also directly challenged the powers that hold people in bondage. When

Jesus taught, things happened in people's lives. A case in point was his teaching in Capernaum. The "new teaching" the people were so dumbfounded by was a *healing*— a casting out of an "unclean spirit." This was not an isolated incident. He was seen as a teacher: when he healed Jairus' daughter (Mark 5:35ff.), when he responded from his depths (literally from the "bowels") to the hungry crowd (Mark 6:34ff.), when he healed the epileptic boy (Mark 9:17ff.), and in many other places. His teaching had true healing power—unlike that of the scribes (Mark 1:22).

It is important to focus on this distinction, because what we really hope for when we return again and again to the scriptures is that we will be touched in the deepest places of ourselves and that something will happen in our lives, as it did in the lives of Jesus' contemporaries. The great temptation is to slip into the scribal style of approaching scripture, partly because we are accustomed to the ascendancy of reason and partly because the scribal approach dampens the potentially discomforting challenge to our self-understanding that can come from an approach more akin to that of Jesus. In our heart of hearts, however, we know that we go to the scriptures— especially the Gospels—hoping to find guidance or to be inspired or to be moved or to be transformed or to be "healed." We go to dictionaries and encyclopedias and history books for information; we go to the scriptures for healing. And if all we use or have at our disposal is the scribal approach to scripture and a set of assumptions similar to that of the scribes, we are virtually guaranteed that that kind of encounter will not take place.

Bultmann tried to raise our consciousness about this.

You cannot talk to someone about life and death, sin and grace, the same way you can inform someone that there are meat-eating plants, or types of fish that bear live offspring. Rather, when we talk to someone about life and death, sin and grace, we are talking about that person's own life, of which all these are an integral part, just as are light and dark, love and friendship. Acknowledging this is the pre-condition of being able to understand; only when we acknowledge this truth can we grasp the message of a text. If we get this, we won't find the text informing us about some curious and previously unknown events; rather the text will disclose to me (new) possibilities of myself. I will be able to grasp these only to the extent that I am open to these possibilities, and will allow myself to be pushed to discover them. I cannot simply accept what has been said as information. Rather if I understand, I have to simultaneously say yes or no to what I have understood. It is not as if I could first understand and only then make a decision about that. Rather I can only understand in an affirming way or in a denying way. For we are talking about the opening up of the possibilities of my own self, which I either understand and embrace as mine, or deny as an undermining of myself. Understanding, therefore, always simultaneously involves decision, taking a stand.[2]

One of the built-in dilemmas of the purely historical-critical approach to scripture can be gleaned from what comes after the hyphen. The word critical, which comes up again and again in describing various methods of research into the New Testament (historical-critical, form-critical, literary-critical, redaction-critical) points to approaches that have in common the intention to judge and analyze what is being looked at. It is a bit like dissecting a frog to find out what is inside. You may know a lot of useful things about the frog thereafter, but you also have a dead frog. This is not to downplay the usefulness of information gleaned from research, which has great value— especially if used properly. I have, however, become painfully aware of how difficult it is to move from a stance that judges and criticizes scripture to one that allows scripture to judge us. The transition is not easy. So what is the alternative? How can an encounter between the Gospels and us become like that between Jesus and those he came in contact with? How can the Gospels have that same kind of healing impact on us? And how can the significant contribution of historical-critical work be made to serve rather than impede that impact?

First we need to remind ourselves that Jesus' encounter with people was just that—from living person to living person. He spoke to or touched people directly. They felt the impact of his authority as a here-and-now living and breathing reality. If we are to recreate that same kind of encounter, either we have to be confronted by a person who has similar healing power and authority or we have to find some way for the scripture to become as real, as alive, as present, and as much a healing resource to us as Jesus was for those people. This latter option is what seems to happen when the method I've been working on is used. I've experienced it many times, both in leadership and in participant roles. But for this approach to be successful, a number of things must happen.

As I said earlier, the word critical is a clue to understanding why the power of scripture has been so blunted for us. To criticize something and then be ready or open to being criticized by it is difficult. Another aspect of this clue is important. The whole atmosphere in which biblical research has been conducted tends to intimidate the "ordinary" person. The wholesale takeover of the scientific mind-set, along with scientific methodology, with its emphasis on facts, objectivity, and rationality, has meant that there must be one right way to interpret a particular biblical passage, and only the experts can truly know what that right way is. Because no one wants to be wrong, there is always apprehension that someone more expert than I will prove me wrong. It is easier to withdraw, to leave scripture alone, or to read it and then talk about something else than to take the risk of being wrong. The atmosphere of biblical research tends to disenfranchise the ordinary person. It is as if a covert hierarchy exists. At the bottom are the laypeople, then come the ordained ministers, then the ministers with Ph.Ds., then the college professors, then the professors at the not-so-prestigious seminaries, then the professors at the more prestigious seminaries, then the young German professors, then the old German professors, and then the Bible, and then perhaps God. When I've talked to people about this issue it has brought smiles of recognition to their faces, but the smiles also reveal the truth of this. We need to free ourselves of the apprehension that has hung over biblical studies, to get out of the competitive stance, if we are to come to the scriptures afresh. It is difficult to be creative, to risk openness, to consider change in a judgmental, competitive atmosphere.

We need to look at our assumptions. If we assume that things like healing or transformation belong in a prescientific, primitive world but not in ours—as do many of the scholars who have worked with scripture (and have taught us the same approach)—the possibility of that happening is radically reduced.

A fact-oriented, rationally based approach does not work when it comes to facilitating healing changes in people's lives. By themselves, facts are not sufficient to motivate us to change. One example is the approach of the schools my children have been attending to the issue of smoking. The schools have done a marvelous job of informing students about the health hazards of smoking cigarettes. They have laid out all the statistics about heart disease, lung disease, cancer risk, and so on. They have shown the students photographs of diseased lungs that exhibit the effects of inhaling cigarette smoke. But as I watch the young people pour out of the high school at the end of the day I see at least six out of every ten reach for cigarettes and light up as soon as they get out the door. The facts have not been enough. Something stronger than the facts is necessary, and until that something is touched, no changes will take place.

A similar phenomenon surrounds the issue of alcohol abuse. The facts about alcohol are also well known—for example, its potential addictive power and the permanent damage it can do to brain cells. But again, the facts are not enough. Something else is more powerful. Most advertisements are sophisticated about parts of that "something else." They proclaim that if you want to have fun, be sexy, be successful, be cool, be manly, be feminine, be beautiful, be sophisticated, have a good time, live the good life, and so on, you ought to drink Blank Brand alcohol. It is as if they were proclaiming aloud the still small voice of alcohol, which whispers to us, "If you want to really live, use me; without me you'll die." This voice is not speaking the fact that "you may become dependent on me and then you will surely die sooner than you would otherwise. Alcoholism is a fatal disease." But such facts alone do not work even when they are seen or heard. What we are looking at here, as in similar kinds of issues in our lives, is a reality that cannot be dealt with by using only the resources of a purely rational approach.

There is, however, an approach that does work for those who become addicted to alcohol. It gives us important clues about what it takes to bring about healing changes in the areas of our lives where it really counts—where we are in the bondage of "evil spirits," be they alcoholism, racism, sexism, handicapism, nationalism, ageism, or whatever. In the alcohol abuse programs with which I am familiar, the presentation of facts about the damaging effects of alcohol is *part* of the treatment. The core of the treatment is a group process aimed at cutting through the rationalizations of the alcoholic, rationalizations that keep the alcoholic from changing. The drinking person sees himself or herself as perfectly rational, even though he or she appears deluded to others. In other words, our rational part can ensnare us in darkness just as easily as it can lead us to enlightenment. The other crucial parts of treatment are the twelve steps of Alcoholics Anonymous. The first two steps are, "We admitted we were powerless over alcohol—that our lives had become unmanageable," and "We came to believe that a Power greater than ourselves could restore us to sanity." One could put a number of things in place of alcohol—food, money, power, success, and so on—but the main point is acknowledging that something has gotten power over us and our reason and that only a Power (exousia) greater than ourselves can restore us to health. What is so important about this model is that it points out clearly that healing takes place only when our inner world is expanded to include a dimension of reality deeper than reason or emotions. ("Evil spirits" distort the emotions as effectively as they distort the thinking process.) Like many other things, alcohol is as much an "evil spirit" as that which had the man in Capernaum in bondage. We still walk under the influence of the "ruler of the authority of the air" referred to in Ephesians 2:2; 3:10; and 6:12, and we still need another authority or power to help us deal with that in moving toward wholeness.

It is almost as if we have to be rescued from our own version of blindness, just as the people in Jesus' day did (e.g., Matthew 23:16ff.). We need to learn to see in a fresh way. During my first summer of fieldwork, I served a small church in West Hartford, Vermont, about eight miles from Hanover, New Hampshire. I discovered that no one in that village had ever been to the campus of Dartmouth College, which is in Hanover. I wanted to take a group of children and adults there, especially to see the Orozco murals in the library's reading room. In preparation for that visit I showed the group some prints of modern art and talked about them. One print was of an abstract drawn by Picasso that portrayed a child surrounded by a visually distorted mother. The visual distortion seemed to convey the mother's tenderness and caring. When I showed the print to the children they quickly and spontaneously said, "Oh, a child and a mother caring for the child." When I showed the same print to the adults they said things like: "What a bunch of crazy lines!" "That's supposed to be a work of art?" "What's it supposed to be anyway?" Not one adult saw the mother or the child. Because the adults could not see what was in the art, they could not catch the feelings intended by the artist as he drew, much less be challenged by the message of the art.

In many ways we are like those adults. We have been trained to look for certain things, to be "objective" and "realistic" and "mature." In the process we have lost part of what we were able to see as children. Perhaps we need to take Jesus' words to heart—we need to become like children if we want to see the kingdom of God. If we cannot see God's kingdom, we cannot respond to it. As Aldous Huxley says,

to be shaken out of the ruts of ordinary perception, to be shown for a few timeless hours the outer and the inner world, not as they appear to an animal obsessed with words and notions, but as they are apprehended directly and unconditionally, by Mind at Large (the Child in us?)—this is an experience of inestimable value to everyone.[3]

One of my favorite children's stories points us to another major area of concern that needs to be dealt with if we are to move to a more satisfying way of using and responding to scripture. The story, which is about the blind men and the elephant, appears in different forms, but I like this poem by John Godfrey Saxe the best:

It was six men of Indostan
   To learning much inclined,
Who went to see the Elephant
   (Though all of them were blind),
That each by observation
   Might satisfy his mind.

21

The First approached the Elephant,
  And happening to fall
Against his broad and sturdy side,
  At once began to bawl:
"God bless me! but the Elephant
  Is very like a *wall!*"

The Second, feeling of the tusk,
  Cried, "Ho! what have we here
So very round and smooth and sharp?
  To me 'tis mighty clear
This wonder of an Elephant
  Is very like a *spear!*"

The Third approached the animal,
  And happening to take
The squirming trunk within his hands,
  Thus boldly up and spake:
"I see," quoth he, "the Elephant
  Is very like a *snake!*"

The Fourth reached out his eager hand,
  And felt about the knee.
"What most this wondrous beast is like
  Is mighty plain," quoth he:
" 'Tis clear enough the Elephant
  Is very like a *tree!*"

The Fifth, who chanced to touch the ear,
  Said, "E'en the blindest man
Can tell what this resembles most;
  Deny the fact who can,
This marvel of an Elephant
  Is very like a *fan!*"

The Sixth no sooner had begun
  About the beast to grope,
Than seizing on the swinging tail
  That fell within his scope,
"I see," quoth he, "the Elephant
  Is very like a *rope!*"

And so these men of Indostan
  Disputed loud and long,
Each in his own opinion
  Exceeding stiff and strong,
Though each was partly in the right,
  And all were in the wrong!⁴

This story felt right the first time I heard it. It reinforced my belief that all of us are blind in some way (John 9:41) and that the Whole Truth is hard to come by. It reminded me of Paul's assertion that we will always (in this life) see dimly and know partially (1 Corinthians 13:12). The story of the blind men and the elephant neatly points out that we are always partly in the right and (partly) wrong at the same time. Truth, like life, is complex. Truth, like life, is not simple.

The Dynamics of Truth and Authority

Until a few years ago I was not fully aware that the story of the blind men and the elephant illustrates one of the four major ways of approaching truth. What made this clearer for me was listening to a minilecture delivered by Thomas Campbell in 1975. I had had hunches about what he presented, but his presentation helped me put them into a clear system. This in turn helped me understand that some of the debate and struggle in the New Testament field results from people working out of different sets of assumptions about truth. And it seemed to me that if this were more widely understood, we could have a less constrained and more faithful dialogue among those seriously interested in scripture.[5]

Each of the four modes of approaching truth starts with an emphasis on one part of the knowing process. In Mode I there is the *Knower*, the person or acting subject in the knowing process. If a system puts its major emphasis here, there will be some major consequences. Because the knowing subject is seen as primary, and because each of us is unique, truth varies from person to person. My truth is not the same as your truth. What works for me may not work for you. Truth is primarily something that is done, and its truth is proven by the fact that it works. Paul Tillich touched on one aspect of this approach in his sermon "Doing the Truth," which is based on John 3:17—

21: "Truth is . . . something which is *done* by God in history, and, because of this, something which is *done* in the individual life."[6] In the dialogue about truth between two "Knowers," the truth of one or the other gains ascendancy. Tillich applies this to Christ when he says: "The decision for or against truth is the life and death decision, and this decision is identical with the decision in which Christ is accepted or rejected. You cannot have an opinion about the Christ after you have faced Him. You can only do the truth by following Him, or do the lie by denying him."[7] In classical philosophy this view was represented by the Sophists. In modern times it is utilized by Martin Heidegger. This mode has the advantage of recognizing the complexity and seriousness of the truth issue. It honors the unique way truth is found in each person and embeds the truth issue in human life, reminding us that the knowing subject is important. It is limited in that there is no truth "out there" to which you and I might jointly be responsible (apart from the way Tillich and others, like Bultmann, use it to refer to the decision for or against Christ as embodying truth). To build an ethic—especially a social one—out of this mode is hard. It can easily become simply "You do your thing and I'll do mine."

All systems for approaching truth include "Knowers," but not all put such a heavy emphasis on the knowing subject. The next system, Mode II, does all it can to downplay the individual Knower's role in the knowing process and focuses instead on the *Knowable*, the immediate object of the knowing subject. Objectivity is this mode's watchword. New Testament scholarship has its primary roots in this mode. Just as the tyranny of dogma and tradition had been challenged by appeal to the scriptures in the Reformation period, so the rigid understanding of scripture was later challenged, this time by a trio of men operating out of this mode: John Locke,[8] Matthew Tindal,[9] and Thomas Chubb.[10] Theirs was a common search for a reasonable, simple gospel that they claimed to find in Jesus himself, in contrast to what they saw as the complicated, subjective interpretations of Paul and of later tradition. Their work with the New Testament revealed to them what they saw as errors within the New Testament, which could be resolved only by reason and objective research, and in turn influenced people like J.S. Semler, J.P. Michaelis, J.J. Griesbach, and H.S. Reimarus, in Germany. Thus the "scientific" investigation of scripture was born.

Mode II was not invented by John Locke and others of his time. It goes back at least to the Greek philosopher Democritus and has probably always been an option in human history. Some of the themes picked up already are characteristic for this mode. Truth is seen as basically simple. The main faculty of the Knower that is utilized in the quest for truth is reason. Reason or rationality or reasonableness is a persistent theme. Emotions are specifically excluded from this system. They interfere with the objectivity needed in the quest for truth. It is fitting that the nuclear research laboratory in Athens is named after Democritus, for his was the first "atomic theory." *Atoma* means "unable to be cut" and refers to Mode II's quest to break down everything into its smallest and simplest component. This system for approaching truth has paved the way for the explosion of information that has made possible everything from an understanding of the formation of the Gospels to the discovery of the atom. It also provides safeguards against the tyranny of unexamined dogma. The limitations of this mode are manifold. To build an ethic out of it is difficult. It tends to be deterministic; each effect has its "natural cause." It is hard-pressed to deal with the whole person, especially the affective and volitional parts, much less the deeper dimensions. It tends to build a false confidence that there are facts in human interactions which are the same as facts about chemical interactions in the inanimate world. Regarding its approach to scripture, one of this mode's most unfortunate effects has been that both fundamentalists and liberals have been equally captivated by it—the fundamentalists claiming that the scriptures are factually true *as is* and the liberals looking for the facts in back of the accounts, both agreeing that truth is basically simple.

In Mode III the emphasis shifts to what is *Known*. What is Known (for sure) are the basic principles or essential truths of each particular discipline. The Knower is downplayed in this mode, as in Mode II, and again an attempt is made to rule out emotions and subjectivity. The complex part of Mode III entails the application of basic principles and essential truths to actual situations and specific problems. Within the Bible it seems that those who come closest to this model are the Pharisees and others for whom the basic challenge was to take a basic truth, such as honoring the sabbath, and apply it to daily life. In classical philosophy the pioneer of this mode was Aristotle. Mode III has the advantage of enabling a community or a discipline to adhere to an agreed-on set of basic principles or truths. One disadvantage is that it can become rigid, and challenges to a long-held set of "knowns" can be seen as threatening to those who have accepted these "knowns." It is easy to forget, for example, that the sabbath was made for people, not people for the sabbath (Mark 2:27), to lose sight of the Knower as much as is the tendency in Mode II.

In Mode IV the emphasis shifts from the Known to *Knowledge*—the whole body of what is known at any given point in time. Once the emphasis is placed here there are also definite consequences. This mode is illustrated by the story of the blind men and the elephant and by Paul's statement in 1 Corinthians 13:12. It assumes there is a truth "out there" that is true in some absolute sense. Our perception of that truth will always be partial because of the limitation of our point of view—whether at any given moment we have the elephant's tail or ear or whatever. The method of expanding our awareness of truth is dialogue; we need to listen to each person's point of view and assimilate it into our total body of *Knowledge*. The six blind men came closer to knowing what the elephant was like by sharing their points of view with one another. It is not that one was right and the others were wrong. All six were partially right and all six partially wrong. Each person had a piece of the truth. In classical philosophy, Mode IV is that of Plato. In church history Augustine represents this mode. In contemporary theology Paul Tillich represents a mixture of this mode and Mode I. One disadvantage of Mode IV is that it can lead to a kind of intellectual game-playing. Right thinking, or consciousness-raising, is seen as preceding right behavior, and the temptation is to be content with and get caught up in the consciousness-raising part. (I can't act yet; I don't know enough.) This mode has many advantages also: It recognizes the complexity of truth in human life; it allows for a kind of playfulness, which fosters creativity and "right-brained" thinking; and it honors the Knower without the anarchic potential of Mode I—there is a truth "out there." Truth is both objective and subjective.

In practice few people represent a pure use of any one mode. As I mentioned, Tillich is an example of the combination of Modes IV and I. He sees this (understandably) also in scripture. He says, for example:

The Greek word for truth means making manifest the hidden. Truth is hidden and must be discovered [Mode IV]. It dwells in the depth, beneath the surface. The surface of our existence changes, moving continually like the waves of the ocean, and it is therefore delusive. The depth is eternal and therefore certain. In using the Greek word [for truth], the Fourth Gospel accepts

27

the Greek concept, but at the same time it transforms it. "Doing the truth," "being of the truth," "the truth has become," "I am the truth"—all these combinations of words indicate that truth in Christianity is something which *happens*, something which is bound to a special place, to a special time, to a special personality [Mode I].[11]

Bultmann is an example of the utilization of Modes II and I—Mode II for his research work *(Sachkritik)* and Mode I for driving home what he saw as the basic challenge of the gospel. Fundamentalists are an example of Mode II-Mode III mix. They hold the truth to be simple—the Bible contains a set of "facts"—but they coalesce around a set of agreed-on Knowns ("the fundamentals").

If diagrammed, the four modes would look like this:

Mode IV
KNOWLEDGE

	K		K	
Mode I	N		N	Mode III
	O		O	
	W		W	
	E		N	
	R			

KNOWABLE
Mode II

All four modes have advantages and disadvantages. Each mode has gained ascendancy at one time or another in the church's history. None of them alone can exhaust the complexity of the biblical witness or of "real life." The main thing I would hope is that we be aware of our assumptions as we search for truth and share our perception of it. A healthy approach is to own what our particular biases are.

My principal approach is Mode IV. That is why I was drawn to the story of the blind men and the elephant. Truth, like life, is complex and elusive, but there is a truth out there that is more than my subjective view of it. Mode IV is especially helpful in Step 1 of my method. At the same time, I recognize the challenge of Mode I; we need to embed truth within the Knower. Mode I is used in Steps 2 to 6, which attempt to integrate the truth discovered in Step 1 into the life of each participant. I acknowledge the usefulness of Mode II as a means of ferreting out needed information, as well as its function as a guard against the subjective excesses of other modes. Mode II is a helpful aid in Step 1, as we look at what any given text has to say on its own terms. Mode III comes into play also, because any given approach—including mine—has a set of assumptions that characterize it. I would be less than candid if I did not admit that I hope my set of assumptions will be shared by others, because I believe these assumptions help restore the living authority of scripture so that it can move us toward wholeness.

CHAPTER II

The Style of Communication as It Affects the Authority of Scripture

During the period I was putting together this method I went through a training program to learn to teach couples how to communicate more effectively.[1] The approach that was taught in the program included a major section on styles of communication, which helped me see that these same styles come into play when we talk with one another about scripture. Two of the styles seemed particularly unsuited to allowing scripture to speak directly to individuals as authority, and two of the styles seemed particularly appropriate in allowing that to happen.

Each of the four styles of communication has its own pull; that is, we communicate in one style or another. In a conversation, it is virtually impossible for one person to stay in one style while someone else is in another style. One style or the other "wins." The same thing goes for a group. A group establishes how it will talk, what style it will use. Even if no one talks directly about the issue, the group establishes which style will be used. Each style is marked by a specific set of intentions, by a distinct set of behaviors, and by how much of ourselves is drawn on and shared with others.

The intention of Style One is to fill in time and keep things moving along smoothly. It is the style used in most common social settings. The behaviors are such things as reporting events, asking and answering routine questions, giving opinions, telling stories. Conversation usually flows from one topic to another without any effort being made to work through any issues, to come to any kind of agreement, or to go much below the surface level of our awareness. Like all other styles, it is useful in the appropriate setting. This style is not aimed at change.

Style Two is a control style. In its lighter form the intentions of Style Two are to direct, persuade, sell, or instruct. In its heavier form the intention is to effect or coerce change in others, or to resist the attempts of someone else to force change in us. It tends to create a win-lose situation, with one person up and the other or others down. In its lighter form its behaviors are giving directions, advising, selling, persuading. In its heavier form, on the active side, the behaviors are labeling ("You're just not trustworthy"), blaming, putting others down; on the passive side, complaining, disqualifying ("That's not what I meant"), playing "poor me," and so on. Style Two draws more on feelings and wants than Style One, but they are not voiced in a self-responsible way. The person speaking does not own his or her thoughts, feelings, or wants, as in statements like "People just don't do things like that" instead of "I do not want you to do that"; or "You make me so mad" instead of "When you do that, I feel angry"; or "No rational person would . . ." instead of "When you do that, I feel . . ." One of the main problems with Style Two, especially in its heavier forms, is that it targets the self-esteem of the other person. The message seems to be from head to head, as it were, but its message tends to hit the receiver in the stomach. This tends to mobilize the defenses of the receiver and prompt another Style Two message, also going to the stomach. And so it goes until the conversation breaks off. When Style Two intentions and behaviors get into the arena of scripture study, they have unfortunate and predictable results. People are unwilling to reveal their real thoughts, feelings, and wants, much less risk trying out new behaviors. Unfortunately, much of scripture study has been contaminated by this style.

One of the clearest examples in my experience occurred several years ago. I attended a week-long conference at which one of the New Testament scholars I had respected from his writings was to appear. While there, I decided to share with him some research I had been doing about Jesus' entry into Jerusalem. I thought he might have some insights that would help me carry my research further, and I thought he might learn something too. So I shared some of my ideas. His response was: "Branscomb thought about that years ago—it was an impossible idea then and still is." That was Style Two. At the time I thought I had two choices—fight back or walk away. I could have fought. I had done my research thoroughly. But I did not want to fight. So I dropped the subject and walked away. I wish now that I had at least said, "Ouch! That feels like a put-down of me!" But like other styles, Style Two is powerful. In this case, it clearly won; my walking away and sulking was also a Style Two behavior—in its passive form.

In contrast to Style Two, which is characterized by a win-lose orientation, Style Three is a win-win way of communicating. It is the way of communicating which fits well into a Mode IV search for truth. There is a suspension of judgment in Style Three that encourages creativity and right-hemisphere thinking. Unlike Style One, where the basic intention is just to keep things moving along, and unlike Style Two, where the basic intention is to control or to force or resist change, the basic intention of Style Three is to put the world on hold for a while while we pause to explore it and reflect on it. It is a searching style that is most akin to what is called brainstorming. It draws primarily on the cognitive dimension, but it allows for the fullest possible use of this dimension. It also serves as a gateway to Style Four. Typical language of Style Three would be: "*I* wonder . . ."; "*I* think . . ."; "*My* hunch is . . . ."

In Style Four the language is also characteristically in the first person. Statements like "I think . . . ," "I feel . . . ," "I want . . . ," "I will . . ." are common. The main difference between Style Three and Style Four is the expansion into all the conscious dimensions of ourselves. Like Style Three, it presumes a nonjudgmental, win-win stance. Style Four, because it taps into all dimensions and because the participants stay self-responsible, provides an atmosphere conducive to change. In this atmosphere we can risk new behaviors that we would otherwise avoid. The freedom fostered by this style makes change possible in a way that the coercive pressure of Style Two never could. Style Two seems to describe a way of relating what Jesus asked us to avoid when he said "Pass no judgement, and you will not be judged. For as you judge others, so you will yourselves be judged [Matt. 7:1–2, NEB]." In the Moving Toward Wholeness Method, I encourage the use of Style Three and Style Four.

In the Prologue, I indicated that the first step in this method involves the use of questions by the leader. At first, this can look to participants like a Style Two type of situation, similar to past school experiences. For many people, past academic experience has left a lingering legacy of anxiety that surfaces when they are asked a question by someone who is seen as taking on a teaching role. The words that would give voice to that feeling of anxiety would be something like "I hope she doesn't call on me because I'm not sure I have the right answer and I'll be so embarrassed if I am wrong." This kind of anxiety is akin to *shame,* or not wanting to look bad to others, and as such it is not conducive to any kind of behavior change, any movement toward wholeness. In fact, it stifles it. The hook that people have, on which to hang this type of anxiety, is the fact that some questions used in this method are indeed intended to call forth basic information and do sound something like school questions. But questions of this kind are simply intended to establish that we have all heard what is actually in a given passage, and to guard against premature projections of ourselves into the passage. Other similar questions are also aimed at facts in the narrower sense. A question such as "Where is Jericho?" would be an example of this. But even at this level of the use of questions, a definite style of leadership is apparent. The leader in this method is not a lecturer, not one who has the truth to pour into those empty vessels who do not have the truth. The leader's basic task is rather to call forth, tug out, elicit the truth that is already there in any given group of people. I have observed again and again that people are surprised at how much truth, how much wisdom, there is just waiting to emerge, just waiting for the right setting and the well-put question.

While there are some simple facts that need to be established (Jericho is not, for example, at the north end of the Sea of Galilee), most of the questions are intended to call forth more than simple facts. For example, as soon as the question is "What was the significance of Jericho in Jesus' time?" we have already a more open-ended question, for which there may be many responses, each of which would probably be partly right and partly wrong. As soon as we move into questions of meaning or significance or judgment about something, or especially anything related specifically to human life, we move into an area where truth becomes more complex. My working assumption is that there is Truth "out there" in some absolute sense, but I also assume that it will always remain at least somewhat elusive. But we *can* approach that Truth. We can come closer to it or move away from it. An important tool in moving closer to it is the well-posed question, which calls forth creative dialogue, which in turn moves us toward the Truth. And as we approach nearer to the Truth in this way, it can be very liberating—the truth does set free (John 8:32). This way of using questions to call forth dialogue in the quest for truth is not in itself anxiety-producing. The atmosphere that develops is one of creative openness and sharing. But if a particular question leads to a piece of truth that is personally challenging, it may trigger some anxiety—but not the unproductive kind associated with shame. In the shame-based anxiety, one's reference point is "What will *they* think of me?" The anxiety that may follow this discovery method is different. The reference point is "What do I think of myself?" or "Am I content staying where I am now that I know _____ about myself?"

There are many precedents for the use of questions as a learning device, the obvious one being Socrates. His trial in 399 B.C.E. was a tribute to the potential power of questions. The "establishment" of Athens found his questions unsettling. They believed that his questions were undermining the unquestioning support they wanted. Socrates, however, defended himself and his duty to pose the difficult questions the Athenian leaders did not want to hear. To them, he was a criminal; in his own eyes, he was a public benefactor. Indeed, good questions can be unsettling—they do push us to new and sometimes uncomfortable insights about ourselves and our world. When this happens, there is always a temptation to silence or turn off the questioner in some way, rather than let the power of the question move us into new and risky territory.

Jesus also used questions to encourage people to grow. When the question "Who is my neighbor?" was posed to him, he responded with a familiar story, but added some new twists. The hero was not a Jewish layperson who responded to the robbed and beaten person with compassion after the "insensitive" Jewish clergy went by on the other side. The hero this time was a stranger, a Samaritan, one of "those people." That was challenging enough. But then came the (new) question: "Which one was neighbor to the person who was robbed and beaten?" (Luke 10:36). So Jesus also used questions as an important part of his teaching. His questioning was also unsettling to the establishment, and he, like Socrates, was silenced—or so it seemed for a while.

We have, then, two different kinds of anxiety that may be produced by questions. The first kind, which we have as a leftover from school days, is a fear of looking bad to the teacher or to some other person we put in a position of authority—something that is seldom growth-enhancing. It is the kind of anxiety produced by Style Two communication. By contrast, the second kind of anxiety is a by-product of discovery about one's self, one's world. This anxiety arises when a question pushes me to see a new truth about myself. As a result, there surfaces some dissonance between what I have been accustomed to seeing in the past and what I now see. The anxiety that arises in this case is *creative anxiety*, and it can be owned and shared by using Style Four. This creative anxiety is part of the energy in us that moves us toward wholeness, that urges us to grow. The focus in the first kind of anxiety is "How can I avoid looking bad to others that I put in authority over me?" The focus in the second kind of anxiety is "Whom do *I* now want to become?"

CHAPTER III

The Dynamics of Being Human

In addressing the question "Whom do I want to become?" there are two major issues, one relating to the New Testament in general and the Gospels in particular, and one relating to our approach to any scriptural text. The first issue has to do with the humanness of Jesus. If we are to look to Jesus in our journey of becoming as our dialogue partner, then we need to ask ourselves to what extent his life too was a journey of becoming. Was Jesus really a human being? The second, related issue has to do with our understanding of the range of human possibilities. What do we human beings look like, and what is involved in the process of human interaction in general?

Turning first to the issue of the humanness of Jesus, the first thing we find is that it is difficult to get back to Jesus the human being. There are many stumbling blocks, including our own preconceptions of what he must have been or what we would like him to have been. The many lives of Jesus, as chronicled by Albert Schweitzer in his book *The Quest of the Historical Jesus*,[1] each of which was intended to be a portrayal of the human being Jesus as he really was, amply show the difficulties involved. Each picture of Jesus turned out to be much like what the author would have seen if he had gazed into a mirror through a pair of rose-colored glasses. These lives of Jesus illustrate what in psychological terms is called *projec-*

tion. Learning about this phenomenon has been helpful for my understanding not just what happens when we attempt to look at the human being Jesus but also what is going on in the incidents in Jesus' life. As I understand the term projection, the place to start is with the assumption that each one of us has the whole range of human possibilities within us that exists in all other human beings. The healthiest stance is simply to acknowledge this, to allow ourselves to be conscious of our solidarity with the rest of the human race. As I once heard Sam Keen put it: "The crazy person says 'I am Buddha *or* I am the Christ *or* I am Hitler *or* I am Adolf Eichmann.' The healthy person says: 'I am Buddha *and* I am the Christ *and* I am Hitler *and* I am Adolf Eichmann.'"

As I heard Sam Keen say this, I felt some sense of anxiety in response to the second sequence. My inner voice wanted to protest, "I am *not* like Hitler." This anxiety is a clue to the phenomenon of projection. What happens is that societal pressures or family pressures or other forces at work in the world around or in us lead us to see certain traits of personality as totally bad or undesirable or inappropriate. These may be traits that in a larger view are actually good and desirable, such as emotional expressiveness in men or assertiveness in women. But if we see these traits as undesirable, where do we put them? We cannot get rid of them altogether (remember, every person always has, at least potentially, all available human attributes). So we suppress them. We drop them into our unconscious.[2] But they do not stay put. These cut-off pieces have an energy of their own. They want out. So if we will not let them come out in a healthy way—come to consciousness and reintegrate or reassimilate them into ourselves—they come out in unhealthy ways. One thing that happens is that we project these undesirable parts of ourselves onto others who, even in some very minimal way, remind us of these unacknowledged parts of ourselves.

Following up on the traits mentioned above, this might sound like this: "Look at that wishy-washy guy over there. How _____!" or "Look at that bitchy woman over there. How _____!" Another common phrase would be: "I would never _____ (like him or her)!" or "I am glad I am not like _____!" as in "I thank thee, O God, that I am not like the rest of men, greedy, dishonest, adulterous; or, for that matter, like this tax-gatherer [Luke 18:11, NEB]." The other possible behaviors that follow on such a projection cast on another would be avoidance of that person or those people, punishment of that person or class in some way, or ostracism of that person or group (casting them out). This kind of projection was operative in the New Testament when people would see Jesus heal and claim that he was inspired by the devil. The claim that Jesus wanted literally to destroy the temple building was probably a similar kind of projection. (That was likely their own unconscious desire.)

But there is another type of projection, which is like the reverse side of the other kind of projection. It is one that has afflicted Jesus from the beginning, and one that affects our access to the human being Jesus. It is always near at hand, especially for us "believers." In this kind of projection, there are certain strengths we wish we had but "know" we never will. Remember, *all* human possibilities are potentially in each of us, but this is not acknowledged. In this case, these wished-for strengths are projected out onto a hero-type figure, be it Jesus or any other person who is cast in a hero-type role. Simultaneously, the undesirable or unwanted traits that are cast onto the other person in the first type of projection are excised in this type. As a result the hero figure becomes stronger and stronger, "purer and purer," more and more exalted, less and less real.

This process began within Jesus' lifetime. We see it, for example, when someone ran up and knelt in front of Jesus and said "Good teacher. . . ." Already this amounts to putting "the good" in some absolute sense into Jesus and suppressing it in the speaker (there is also an implied demand: "You'd better be good or else"). Jesus seemed to sense that, for he replied, "Why do you call me good? No one is good except God alone. [Mark 10:17–18, RSV]." Between the earlier and later Gospels, we see the same process at work. One example is the story of the healing of Bartimaeus, the blind beggar, which is found in Mark and in Matthew and Luke. In Mark, the earliest Gospel, we find the following details. Bartimaeus is asked to come to Jesus; he throws off his garment, springs up, and goes to Jesus on his own. After Bartimaeus receives his sight, Jesus tells him that it is his (Bartimaeus') faith that has made him whole (or saved him; *sodzein* is translated both ways). In Matthew and Luke, both of whom had Mark in front of them when they wrote, a variety of things happen to the story. In Luke, Bartimaeus loses his name and becomes simply "a blind man." In Matthew, he also becomes anonymous, but a second anonymous person is added. In Matthew "they" are still asked or called, whereas in Luke he is commanded to be led to Jesus. In Luke, Jesus still tells him that his faith has "moved him toward wholeness," but in Matthew, Jesus makes no mention of their faith or anything about wholeness; they receive their sight simply because Jesus was moved to make that happen. (See Mark 10:46–52; Matthew 20:29–34; Luke 18:35–43.) What we see at work here is obvious. While Jesus becomes more exalted and more powerful, Bartimaeus loses his identity and becomes more lowly and more passive.

But the same thing already at work in the Gospels themselves has happened ever since, even among liberal scholars. One example of this is what commentators have tried to do with the story in Mark 11:12–14, where Jesus curses a fig tree because it had no fruit (even though it was not the season for it to have fruit). This action is difficult to incorporate into an overly exalted view of Jesus, so various attempts have been made to excise it or explain it away. This is the case even though Mark says specifically that the disciples heard Jesus say it (something that is not common) and even though there is no a priori reason why Jesus could not have said it. One scholar may be taken as representative of others when he writes:

This is one of the most curious stories about Jesus and one which most obviously [sic] cannot be taken as sober history. Jesus scarcely went about blasting fruit trees simply because they did not have fruit ready for him at the moment. Mark explains that, being Passover time, it was not the season of figs, which, of course, makes the act more unreasonable [sic]. A considerable amount of scholarly energy has gone into an attempt to save the situation . . . [but] it still remains nonsensical and "out of character" for Jesus to have forbidden the tree to have any fruit in the future simply because it did not have any at the moment.[3]

The key word in this commentary is "unreasonable." Indeed, it is not "reasonable." But it is understandable—all the more so when we consider the context. According to Mark, the incident occurs between Jesus' scouting expedition to the temple area (Mark 11:1–11) and his return on the next day to clear the temple area (Mark 11:15–19). Surely this was one of the most emotion-packed times in Jesus' life. And if we take the incarnation seriously, if the Word was truly made *flesh* (John 1:14), if Jesus was indeed human, then this is an understandable reaction in that situation. Just about everyone, in a time of stress, has run into a table leg and cursed the table for being in the wrong place at the wrong time or some similar action, so why not accept that Jesus could also have done that? Because *we* usually feel foolish afterward and we do not

41

want our heroes to feel foolish or to do something they would later regret. It is too human.*

In *Questions Are the Answer*, I dealt with the effects of this kind of projection, and I'd like to quote a part of chapter 7 of that book:

A hero is someone to whom we say, "Oh how I wish I could be perfect like her or like him!" The catch here lies in the (often silent) tag to this sentence: "But I know I never can be." Relating to someone as a hero then, rather than empowering me to move toward my God-given uniqueness, tends to do the opposite by giving me an unattainable ideal over and against which I carry around a depressing or paralyzing sense of guilt. . . . So relating to Jesus *simply* as a hero would imply that far from this relationship being empowering and growth-enhancing, it would do the exact opposite.

So what is the alternative? The starting point is to approach Jesus without fixed expectations, images, titles—to come to him with the same kind of openness and willingness to be surprised or challenged that you would bring to a relationship with any other human being. You wouldn't approach someone and say to that person, "Please sum up who you are in an image or title so I'll know how to relate to you." That kind of approach closes rather than opens up genuine dialogue.

The key which opens up the alternative of genuine openness is contained in the assertion of the Gospel accounts that indeed Jesus was a human being in the fullest sense of the word. In fact, the Gospels came into being as a way of counteracting the opposite assertion—that Jesus was only seemingly human, that he was a kind of ghostly figure—either less or more than human, depending on how you look at it. Even the Gospel of John, which has the most ethereal presentation of Jesus, states emphatically, "And the Word became *flesh*" (John 1:14, RSV, italics added).

At the most basic level this means that Jesus shared the same kinds of feelings and experiences and seeming limitations you and I know to be a part of our life. He got angry (Mark 10:14). He experienced sadness (Luke 19:41), as well as joy (Luke 15:6;

---

*Webster defines human as "susceptible to or representative of the sympathies and frailties of [human] nature." *Webster's New Collegiate Dictionary* (Springfield, Mass.: G. & C. Merriam Co., p. 556).

John 15:11; John 17:13). He enjoyed good food and wine (Matthew 11:19). He wasn't always sure what it was God wanted him to do and had to pray for guidance, sometimes with loud cries and tears in his eyes (Hebrews 5:7), sometimes praying all through the night (Luke 6:12). He was often misunderstood by countless people, including his hometown folks (Mark 6:3–6). He could unwittingly say harsh things that he later regretted (Matthew 15:22–28). And at times it seemed *nobody* understood him, not even his closest friends (Mark 8:17–18).[4]

So much is at stake in being willing to see Jesus as fully human. The experiences of early researchers of the life of Jesus should serve as a warning to us in this regard. They thought that if they could get back to Jesus himself, to Jesus the human being, they would find a simple, reasonable person behind the complex theologizing of Paul and the later church. In fact, the opposite is true. Even though we will never get back to the "real Jesus" (unencumbered by anybody's reaction to him), the closer we get to him, the more complex he becomes. It is the later portrayals that are purer and simpler. Jesus of Nazareth, like any other human being, was complex. Like other humans, he had to struggle to understand, to puzzle about the future, to learn from his mistakes. He was not set down on earth already whole.* He too had to move toward wholeness. And I believe this is good. I can be in a more creative and challenging dialogue with someone who has gone through the same kind of journey of becoming that characterizes my life than I could with someone who had everything together from the start.

So in this method, I operate out of the assumption, based on my understanding of two centuries of historical-critical studies of the Gospels as well as the psychological

---

*As it says in the Letter to the Hebrews 5:8–9, "Even though he was a son, he learned obedience through the things that happened to him, and having become whole, he became the source of wholeness for all time" (my translation).

dynamics of projection, that Jesus of Nazareth was fully human. I simply ask that you try that out as a working assumption as we look at the narratives of Jesus' life together. I do not ask people to accept my assumptions. I just want to be up front about what my assumptions are and ask that participants play along with them for the duration of the seminar or weekend. My experience has been that people find this to be a freeing, liberating way to approach the Gospel accounts. Comments of two past seminar participants might serve as examples:

The most important learning for me was the humanness of Jesus—he was far more "human" on earth than I had previously thought. *This protects and elevates my humanness* [italics added].

The most important learning for me was zeroing in on Jesus' human (and dark) side. I need to consciously remind myself of his humanness because all my life he has been "glorified" out of existence. Remembering his human side helps me to feel better about myself.

We have been looking at the issue of the humanness of Jesus and what that means in terms of what we might be looking for or open to when we look at the records of Jesus' life. Related to this is a broader issue: What are we humans like, and what is involved in any given human interaction? This is important, because our understanding of the dynamics of human life will affect what we are looking for in scripture as well as what we are open to in ourselves.

For example, Thomas Jefferson was convinced that it was reason that distinguished human beings from the rest of creation and was therefore suspicious of anything that hinted of "emotionalism" or "irrationality." This led him to make up his own edited version of the Gospels. In this version, which he read daily, he included only those portions of the Gospels which he considered to be rational and excluded all the miracles and any other portions that showed Jesus to be less than totally reasonable.

Like Jefferson, each of us has some model of what human life involves, whether we are aware of it or not, and this influences what we are prepared to find and will find in scripture as well as what we are likely to avoid or not even see in scripture. A unidimensional model, like Jefferson's, yields a unidimensional scripture, one from which much will be automatically excised. It also limits the impact scripture can have on us. A more complex model does more justice to the complexity of life and of scripture. It also is more likely to allow the scriptures to impact us in a significant way.

In the recent past, people in the field of biblical scholarship have tended to be suspicious of the use of psychological insights because of the excesses of some who have misused psychology. But the choice is not whether or not I will use psychological insights. The choice is rather how conscious I will be of the psychological insights that I inevitably use. If we look at the example of Thomas Jefferson this becomes abundantly clear. The field of psychology as such had not even come into being in Jefferson's time, but he did have a psychology, an understanding of what human beings are like. And this understanding—this psychology—dramatically influenced what Jefferson did with scripture. The same is true of everyone, including biblical scholars. We all have an understanding of human life, a psychology, that influences everything we do—including our study of scripture. So it is important to be as conscious and articulate as possible about our understanding of the human, for only then can we be in dialogue with one another about this issue that affects the whole task of biblical research and biblical interpretation.

The model of human interaction that I have developed

has been evolving over many years, and it continues to evolve. One major step along the way for me was becoming familiar with the model developed by Sherod Miller and his colleagues.[5] Their work is based, in turn, on the work of many other behavioral scientists, most of whom I had studied before. But their model started to put things together for me in an especially helpful and clear way. Other major influences have been the work of Carl Jung and, most important, the New Testament itself.

In order to focus on each part of the model of human interaction, I will build the diagram of the model one piece at a time and describe each piece as we go along. In Diagram—1, each side of the circle represents one person.

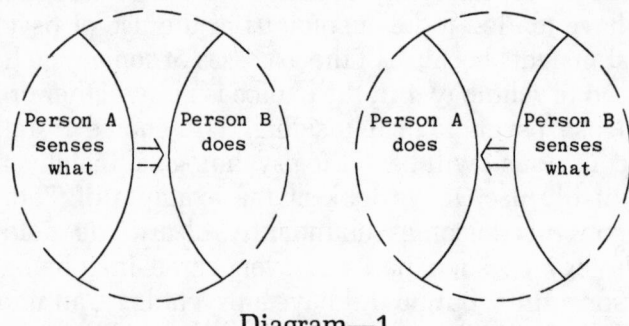

Diagram—1

The dotted lines of the circle refer to the border between what is out in the open, as it were, in any given interaction between people, and what is hidden. I want to explore the part within the dotted lines first. The "do" dimension contains the words a person actually uses, the tone of voice, facial expressions, posture, and other nonverbal expressions, such as clenching one's fist or reaching out. It also includes all other physical aspects of a person, like dress or hair color and arrangement. This is the dimension of "facts" in human interaction. The word fact comes from the Latin word *facere*, which means "to do" or "to make." The same Latin word is the source of the word face and the word facade. These "facts" are the *only* parts of a person that are out in the open for the sensory system of another person to pick up. This may seem like common sense, but a good deal of confusion results in human communication when we mix up what we see, for example, with what we think about or how we interpret what we see. So it is crucial to realize that our sensory systems pick up *only* what we actually see, hear, touch, taste, and smell. Even at this level, the process of interaction between two people can become complex. The interaction actually looks more like Diagram—2.

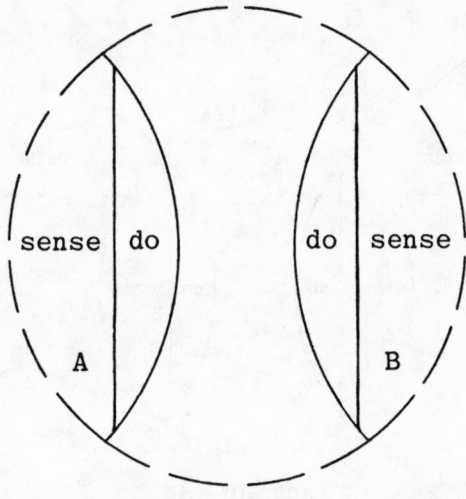

Diagram—2

We normally are aware of or sense only part of all the signals we are sending to another person. I may be wrinkling my brow, for example, and not be aware of it. Or my voice may be louder or softer than I realize. In this case, the only way for me to know that is for the other person to tell me. Also, my actions may hinder my capacity to sense what another person is saying or doing. For example, another person may be halfway through a sentence before

47

I hear what that person is saying, because the focus of my awareness is elsewhere. We routinely shut down parts of our awareness in order to focus on one part of what is happening in the world. If you shifted your awareness right now to pick up *all* the sounds that are in the air, there would be more sounds out there than you were aware of previously. So even in this area within the dotted lines, communication is complex.

This part of human interaction becomes even more complex when we add the thinking or cognitive dimension, as in Diagram—3. Whatever actions I sense in

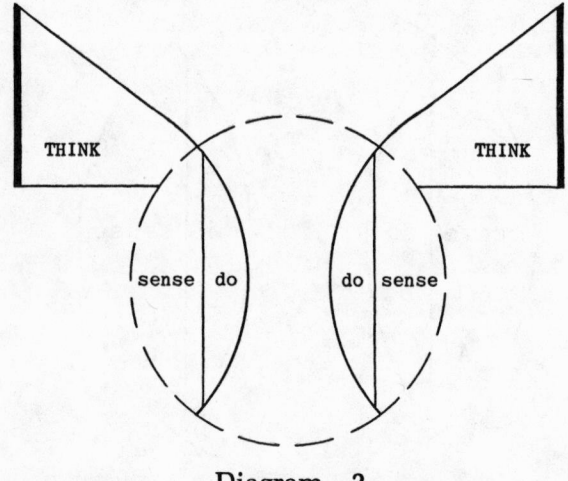

Diagram—3

another are always interpreted. I *think* about what they mean. Take the nonverbal clue of a wrinkled forehead. I may see and think that it means you are confused or puzzled, but it may simply be what you do when you are concentrating (that is, neither confused nor puzzled). The only way you can know what I think your behavior means, and the only way I can know what you are thinking, is for us to reveal that to one another. The thinking (or cognitive) part of us is therefore a hidden dimension of ourselves, until we choose to reveal it. This part of us is made more complex because I may be only partially aware of what I am thinking (as in daydreaming).

One major source of confusion is the mixing of thinking statements and sense statements. I might see someone else's wrinkled forehead and say, "You look confused." That sounds like a sense statement, a report of what I see in the other person. But it is not. It is my thought about what I see. A more accurate statement would be, "I see you wrinkling your forehead. I'm thinking you might be confused." Another source of confusion occurs when someone makes a thinking statement that is either the opposite of what the person is really thinking or gives voice to only one part of the person's thinking (a "facade"). Thinking about these sources of confusion is important not just for our understanding of our communication process; but also because they serve as a caution when we "hear" someone say something in scripture. For example, when the woman comes in and anoints Jesus' feet, Jesus' host says to himself, "If this fellow were a real prophet, he would know who this woman is that touches him, and what sort of woman she is, a sinner [Luke 7:39, NEB]." That is what he says he is thinking. Inside, he (and the other guests) might be thinking other things, for example, "Why isn't she doing that to us?" "It would be OK somewhere else, but not out here in the open where everyone can see"; "She knows too much about us. I wish she would go away before she says something." So it is important to remember that our thinking is a hidden dimension of ourselves that only comes out to the extent that we are aware of what we are thinking and choose to reveal it truthfully.

Recently there has been much creative work that shows two different ways of cognitive functioning which can be traced to different halves of the brain. Walter Wink has an excellent presentation on this in his recent book.[6] I have also found a study from the field of art to be very stimulating in this regard.[7] As the author says, "The left hemisphere (which controls the right side of the body) analyzes, abstracts, marks time, plans step-by-step procedures, verbalizes, makes rational statements based on logic."[8] With the right hemisphere, which controls the left side of the body (where our hearts are), "we 'see' things that may be imaginary. . . . We see how things exist in space and how parts go together to make up the whole. Using the right hemisphere, we understand metaphors, we dream, we create new combinations of ideas."[9] So we can see that we need to be aware of and cultivate our use of both kinds of thinking. We especially need to be challenged to develop our right-brain functioning—because this has tended to be suppressed, because it gives us access to a realm of truth that would otherwise be closed off, and because so much of the biblical material utilizes metaphors and the like (what I call "is-like thinking") as in "The kingdom of God . . . is like a grain of mustard seed [Mark 4:30–31, RSV]."

But even as we absorb the insights these distinctions point to, we need to remember that we are still looking at cognition, at thinking. We are not looking at feelings, even though feelings do seem to be associated more with the left side of the body and to be registered mainly in the right hemisphere. Feelings are something quite different from thoughts. Thoughts are in the head; feelings are mostly somewhere else in the body. The second "hidden" dimension then, in any given interaction, is the feeling (or affective) part. We now turn to Diagram—4.

Feelings or emotions are among the most misunderstood dimensions of ourselves. Feelings are neither good nor bad, neither positive nor negative. Feelings are simply our temporary and spontaneous body responses to what is happening in us and around us. They frequently come about in response to a gap between what we think will happen and what actually happens. I may think

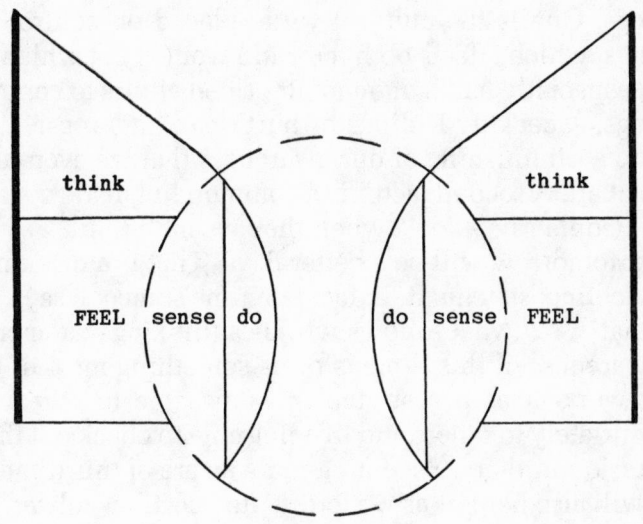

Diagram—4

someone will be kind to me, so when they act otherwise I feel hurt, then angry. Or I may think someone will be unkind to me, so when they act otherwise I feel happy. Feelings are like barometers in us—they tell us about something else that's going on in us and/or around us. They are valuable, God-given clues to which we need to pay attention. Sometimes we hear the phrase "You shouldn't feel_____." This is not a valid comment, because feelings just happen. The ethical implications come only in how we choose to act or not act on them.

However, feelings are a hidden dimension too, because any given behavioral signal by someone else may not reveal the real feeling of that person. Someone may say to me, "I hate you!" (the "facade"), but what that person may be feeling is fear because she or he thinks I don't like her or him. So the only way I can truly know how another actually feels is for that person to reveal it to me, and vice versa. This presupposes, of course, that the other is aware of what she or he is actually feeling.

Many factors tend to diminish our awareness of our

feelings. One is the cultural value placed on control of feelings, which affects both men and women but which is often especially harsh on men. Repeated efforts to control feelings, especially feelings of hurt, fear, and anger, can lead to a diminishing of our awareness that we even feel them at all. A second factor is a common linguistic confusion. People say "I feel" when they mean "I think," as in "I feel tomorrow will be a better day." That is a thinking, not a feeling, statement. In fact, anytime someone says, "I feel that . . . ," what follows will be a thinking statement. So awareness of this dimension is something most of us must work at as a first step in being able to reveal it appropriately to others and in being able to check out that dimension in them. Becoming more aware of this dimension will also help us as we formulate questions related to feelings in Step 1.

Because feelings are such a misunderstood and suppressed dimension, I have developed a checklist of feelings, which you'll find in Appendix I. This is an extensive list, but I have become convinced that the feelings listed are mostly variations of three basic primary emotions and one secondary emotion. There is the primary "soft" feeling of joy, which is our body's response when we perceive things going well for us. There is the primary "hard" emotion of pain, which at the physical level indicates injury of some kind to the body and at the cognitive level indicates that we think we have been "put down" or are sustaining some other kind of psychologically injurious condition. There is the primary "hard" emotion of fear, which is our body response to anticipated injury (and pain), whether to the body itself or to our sense of self-worth. Each of these emotions has many words that describe nuances of them. For example, anxiety is a relatively modest amount of fear; panic is a lot of it. Embarrassment is one kind of pain; humiliation is another.

Then there is the secondary emotion of anger, perhaps

the least understood of all feelings. Anger is the emotional energy we put into our behavior in response to feeling fear or pain. It says, "I've been hurt" or "I'm afraid! I do not like it! I want some change!" Like other feelings, anger is neither good nor bad, neither positive nor negative. It just is. It is "good" in the sense that it is God-given, but its ethical implications come only when anger is expressed. It can be expressed constructively, in a way that does not attack the self-esteem of the other person, or it can be expressed destructively.

So the second important dimension of ourselves that we need to be aware of and understand is the affective, or feeling, dimension. Feelings are our body responses to what is going on around us or within us. They are, however, *ours*. No one can make us feel either good or bad. What one person experiences as hurtful, another person may experience as pleasant. So our feelings are indeed ours. We are, however, not responsible for what feelings we experience—they happen so spontaneously. What we are responsible for is how we express them and act on them.

It is important to add that we can change over time in the way we think or interpret some part of life, and that this will trigger a different set of feelings. For example, I grew up in a family whose political allegiance was strongly conservative and Republican. Absorbing this, when I saw a liberal Democratic candidate I tended to feel suspicious (somewhat fearful). Somewhere in my midtwenties my political views underwent a shift to the left, and I no longer felt suspicious of liberal politicians. So feelings do change; they are temporary, body responses. They are like warning lights on the dashboard of a car. They are signals pointing to something else, and each points to something different. For example, anger points us to our third hidden dimension, to our wants.

The third hidden aspect then, is the wanting (or volitional) part of ourselves, as illustrated in Diagram—5.

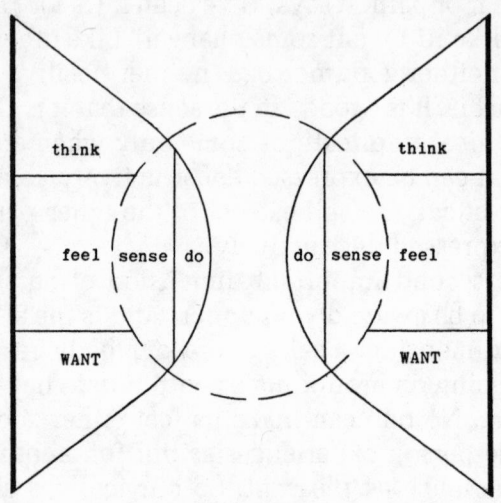

Diagram—5

This wanting is sometimes called our "intentions" or what we "mean" as in "I didn't mean (or intend) this, I meant (or intended) that." My children used to use this a lot, as in "I didn't *mean* to hit my sister, I was just stretching." What he *did* was hit her. *She's* sure he did mean (intend, want) to hit her. *He* says no. There is, however, no way for her to dispute his "real" intentions, for they are known only to him, unless he chooses to reveal them (assuming that he is aware of them).

Like feelings, wants not only start out hidden, they often remain hidden, because we have frequently been discouraged from having or, and especially, from revealing them in the past. For example, "Mommy, I *want* an ice-cream cone!" "No, you don't, besides you should say 'Please may I' not 'I *want!*' Anyway, what you really want is a carrot. It's better for you." And so it goes. We are discouraged from voicing our real wants, so we tend to get out of touch with them, and others often do not know where we are coming from. But our wants are important.

They are the energy source that mobilizes our behavior, and any creative change in our behavior flows almost always from our want energies and not from our "shoulds" or "oughts" or whatever.

We do not act, sense, think, feel, and want in a vacuum. There is always more to it. We are always acted on by those forces that are pointed to by the words and images in the area behind the bold vertical lines in Diagram—6.

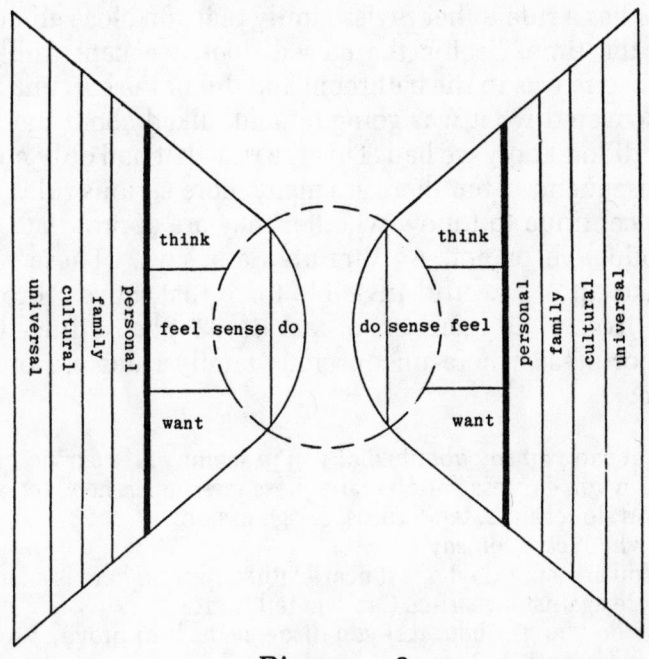

Diagram—6

This area of the model has many layers. The first layer is our personal unconscious—things that we have forgotten but that are still retrievable, things that have slipped into our unconscious, and things that we have suppressed. For example, I may prize honesty, so the lying me may be stored in my personal unconscious. There is also an unconscious specific to family groupings. In fact, the work done in this area is illuminating for all the others. Pieces of family life that most families are not conscious of are the rules they live by. Most people can easily state some of the rules, like "Don't chew with your mouth open." But there are also submerged rules. We had a Swiss exchange student with us this year, and we discovered many of our unconscious rules because she did not act in accordance with them. For example, we apparently have a rule that you leave the bathroom door open when no one is in it, so you'll know that no one is in it. She has a rule in her Swiss family that you close all doors all the time. Seeing the closed door, we kept thinking someone was in the bathroom and did not use it, until we discovered what was going on and talked about the rule we didn't know we had. This is a rule that had only minor consequences, but there are many more serious rules that we continue to follow whether they are appropriate and productive or not. As Virginia Satir says, "These rules make up a powerful invisible force that moves through the lives of all members of families."[10] She outlines four major areas where unconscious family rules are operative:

What can you say about what you're seeing and hearing?
Can you express your fear, helplessness, anger, need for comfort, loneliness, tenderness, or aggression?
To whom can you say it?
You are a child who just heard father swear. There is a family rule against swearing. Can you tell him?
How do you go about it if you disagree or disapprove of someone or something?
If your seventeen-year-old son reeks of marijuana, can you say so?
How do you question when you don't understand (or do you)?
Do you feel free to ask for clarification if a family member doesn't make himself understood? Is your rule if YOU don't understand ME, it is always because of YOU?"*

---

*Reprinted by permission of the author and publisher. Virginia Satir, *Peoplemaking*, Science & Behavior Books, 1972. Pp. 98–99.

Rules in this area are not necessarily bad. We cannot help but have rules. As soon as people start living or working together, they spring into being. The only question is, how conscious of them will we be, and are they healthy? This layer of the unconscious is all the more complex because we have not only rules but also rules about the rules. In my family of origin, we had an unspoken rule— "We do not talk about sex." We also had an unspoken rule about that rule—"We do not talk about why we do not talk about sex." This layer is behind or underneath the personal unconscious because it affects what we will have in our personal unconscious and our ability to retrieve pieces from it.

The next layer, back or down, is the unconscious that is specific to the culture in which we live. When you live in another culture for an extended period of time, as I did in Scotland, you discover many of the rules of the culture you are living in, as well as of your own culture. A friend of ours left her baby in a carriage outside a building while she went in for a short while. As she came out, she saw a Scottish woman reaching into the carriage and picking up her baby. She asked the woman what she was doing, and she replied, "I am turning her over on her back. She'll suffocate lying on her stomach." Our friend said, "But back home we always put babies on their stomachs and they do not suffocate." The Scottish woman replied with great indignation, "Well, you're in Scotland now!" This example shows the power of the widely accepted but unconscious rules and rule systems of a culture, which get embedded in each person's unconscious and stay there until retrieved in some way. In this layer are all the "isms," like sexism, racism, handicapism. This area affects both our family system unconscious and our personal unconscious. All three influence and can determine our behavior unless brought to consciousness.

There is also a deeper layer—what Jung calls the "collective unconscious." This part of our unconscious seems to be similar in all people across cultural groups. Certain symbols and images appear in dreams and in religious documents all over the world and seem to be part of this "collective unconscious." The phenomenon of extrasensory perception operates in this area. Here too are the forces the Bible refers to as principalities and powers, angels and demons. This whole unconscious dimension is so important because through it comes our access to God—or God's access to us. But it is also from this dimension that most of the crazy or destructive behaviors that we see emerge. Out of this whole unconscious dimension come healing and new growth, as well as that which hinders healing and new growth. The main point is that we are influenced by it, like it or not. If we try to ignore it, it will influence us anyway, often in destructive ways. If we

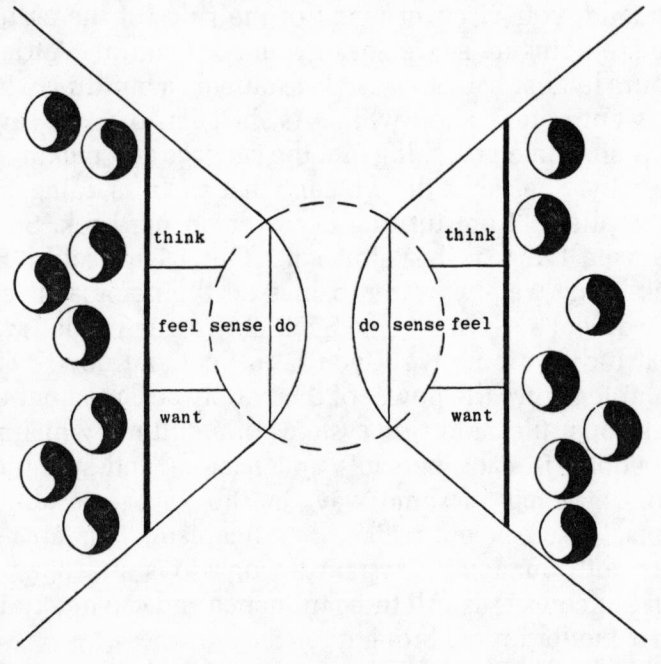

Diagram—7

choose to pay attention to it, then the healing power it contains can emerge and we can move to greater personal and interpersonal wholeness.

When I was developing the diagram of the model of human interaction and searching for some way to symbolize what I was coming to understand about the different pieces of our unconscious, I came up with circles that were half light and half dark (see Diagram—7). This seemed an appropriate way to show that these pieces of our unconscious have a light and a dark side, just as the pieces of our conscious have. Take the cluster of ideas that revolve around the male and female roles. In and of itself, it is not bad for a family, or a whole culture, to have a set of expectations about male and female roles. For example, the expectation that men don't cry probably goes back to a time when men were expected to be ready to defend their families and, if necessary, to kill. It is difficult to carry out this demanding role if you do not have emotional self-control. But the situation in which this may have been appropriate (even if regrettable) is no longer with us. Now this same expectation, which at one time may have been in the light side of the circle (i.e., served a useful function) is in the dark side (i.e., is detrimental to the psychological health of men). It has become destructive.

This piece of sexism, like the others, has been passed on from generation to generation and, like the other forces represented by the circles, it has a lot of power. When I was nine years old, I was beaten up by the neighborhood bully. I was really hurt and was still crying when I arrived home. But the power of the sexism circle got to me, and my sense of shame was so strong that I resolved never to cry again. I knew that if I was to grow up to be a "real man" I would never give in again to this sign of weakness. As I grew up I stuck by this decision except for a rare bit of backsliding—usually about once a year. But when I felt "it" coming, I would make a dash for some private place where no one would see or hear me. It was not until I was thirty years old that this piece of sexism was seriously challenged for me, when I attended my first training lab or encounter group. In this setting I saw men cry and not feel ashamed. In fact, they seemed to feel better afterward. I heard people talk about feelings as normal and important, even for men. I was encouraged to get in touch with what I was feeling and to express it then and there—in the group. I was encouraged to challenge the old rule and adopt a new one—"Human beings cry, and men are human." It took time, but the dam broke, and I cried and cried and cried. There were a lot of stored-up tears to come out. It was very releasing and very healing.

This shows just how these pieces from behind the bold vertical lines actually work and something of what it takes to get freed of the negative side of their influence. It takes a lot of consciousness-raising to drag them out of the unconscious part of ourselves into the open where they can be dealt with in a creative way. Even then they give up their power very slowly, and it is easy to regress. To stay with the above example, I now cry more easily, but I am still influenced by the part of sexism that says, "Men don't cry!" Feelings of shame still lurk around when I feel like crying. I also still tend to react differently when I see men cry than when I see women cry. (It's OK for women to cry—it's part of their "nature.") We need to recognize that the "isms" have a lot of power and that we must deal with them if we hope to grow as persons, if we are to become less constrained in our behavior, if we are to move toward wholeness.

The one part of the diagram I have not discussed is God. This does not reflect a belief that God is a postscript to human life or is found *only* at this point. Indeed, there is no area of life where God's presence cannot be discerned. In the Complete Diagram of Human Interaction, I

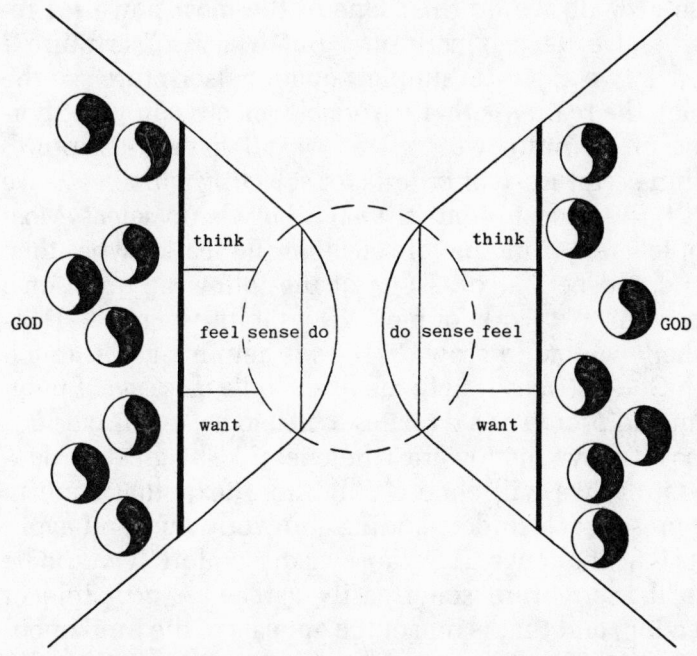

Complete Diagram of Human Interaction

have put God at the points indicated to show something
that reflects both my reading of the New Testament and
my own experience: Our access to God has to go through
the intervening space where the circles are. If these pieces
behind the bold vertical lines remain in our unconscious
and are not brought to consciousness, they clutter up the
space through which God has to move to get to us or
through which we have to move to get to God. Con-
versely, the more cleared out this space becomes, the
more open becomes our access to God, and vice versa—
and the more clearly the presence of God can be seen in
life. So getting at the things behind the bold vertical lines
becomes even more vital, because only this way can we
get more fully in touch with the wellspring of all healing,
all wholeness, God.

So how do we do this? One of the most powerful resources we have is scripture. But what is "scripture"? Even if we make a simple equation (scripture = the Bible), the reality is that we are all selective in what portions of scripture we utilize. We all have a scripture-within-scripture. Our criteria for selecting which texts we will turn to most often will vary, but we do select. Most people's real principle of selection (no matter what they say) could be stated as one of the following questions: "Does this text work for me?" "Does it inspire me?" "Does it challenge me to grow?" "Does it help me get in touch with God?" "Does it help me hear God's message of judgment and promise as it relates to me, to us, to our world?" "Does it move me toward wholeness?" The greatest danger is that we will choose only those texts that confirm our present self-understanding and worldview and avoid texts that challenge us or cause us discomfort. It would be nice if there were some easily agreed-on principle of selection, and that is one of the appeals of the fundamentalist stance, that every portion of the Bible is literally true. But for those of us who do not accept that principle, no other equally simple principle can be formulated. The best we can do is listen respectfully to those who put the Bible together and not close ourselves off prematurely to the possibility of any text therein becoming "scripture" for us—that is, a text that "works," challenges us to grow, and so on. It may well be that the very text we have written off may be the one we need most to listen to in our particular faith journey.

For scripture to have a genuine impact on us we need also to come to it with a dual awareness. We need to be sensitive to all the dimensions of human interaction that we have been looking at, both in the text and in ourselves, and we need to be ready to be challenged in all these dimensions. Even if we expand our approach to scripture beyond the confines established in liberal circles of left-hemisphere thinking and expand it to include right-hemisphere thinking, that is not enough. We have to look at our affective, our volitional, conscious dimensions as well as our cognitive dimensions. We also have to include our personal, family, cultural, and collective unconscious dimensions. And then we still need to look at the "So what?" question. We need to incorporate the new insights gained into new behavior (Matthew 7:15–20). The truth sets free for a purpose—for a new way of acting in the world.

CHAPTER IV

The "Moving Toward Wholeness" Method of Using Scripture

We have been so accustomed to an atmosphere of debate and competition in scripture study, especially in academically oriented circles, that there is still a part of us that wants to look for the one right answer. This may be the case with the present method, even though we hear assurances that this is a more-than-one-right-answer approach. So when the leader asks a question, we still suspect that she or he is just waiting for "it"—the right answer.

One way to counteract this is to utilize the diagram of human interaction presented in Chapter III. Looking at this diagram, we can see why there cannot be one right answer to so many of the important questions that need to be addressed. Let's take one sensory signal—tears—as an example. Just think for a moment what tears could signify—sadness, joy, anxiety, relief, sympathy for another person, an irritant in your eyes, and a hay fever reaction, among other things. In this example, we are talking about a clear, visually verifiable behavioral signal. If we move to verbal signals that seem to reveal the hidden dimensions of thoughts, feelings, and wants, things are no less complex. Let's take the verbal signals "I hate you. I think you're a jerk. I want you to leave." These may be outward signals that match what is going on inside the sender of

64

the signals, but what may really be going on inside the person could be this: "I love you. I'm not sure you really love me. I'm afraid you'll leave if things get tough, so I might just as well test this out right now."

So as soon as we move from behavioral signals to what is behind them (the hidden conscious dimensions), things get complicated. When we move to the *unconscious* dimensions, that is even more true. In a dialogue today, we can at least reveal to one another what we are really feeling, thinking, and wanting (to the extent we are aware of it), and we can work at the unconscious part in some direct ways. But when we come to a biblical passage, we can only use our best efforts at creative imagination and voice our hunches about what those hidden dimensions might be. This is where we need one another in a group—in a brainstorming atmosphere—to come up with as many hunches as we can about what is in the hidden dimensions behind what we sense in the scripture. It is important to make this effort, because only when we come to have some appreciation for these dimensions in the text can the text come alive and a person-to-person type of encounter take place. Only when this happens are we truly challenged and pushed to grow through our encounter with scripture.

Step 1 in this method of Bible study is what I call *active listening*. The goal of this step is to get inside the text as fully as possible on its *own* terms. We are not seeking to find out what it "means," nor are we, at this stage, trying to find out what we can learn from it. The ideal setting is a small group of anywhere from twelve to twenty. When the group is smaller than twelve, people tend to get too invested in their ideas, and the playful, brainstorming style needed for Step 1 is more difficult to sustain. When the group is larger than twenty, it is difficult to involve so many in the process.

The group will gather with a number of expectations.

There might be expectations that are a residue of school experiences, or there might be another set of expectations, which are a carryover from encounter groups or other "growth" groups where participants give and receive feedback from each other. The latter set of expectations is likely to be triggered by what people have heard and assumed about the method or by the way I recommend the group be set up—in a circle.

In a growth group or encounter group, the people are seated in a circle so that each person can give face-to-face feedback to another. This kind of feedback can be helpful in that kind of setting, but *not* in this. In my method the circle is used as a visible symbol of wholeness. It also enables each participant (including the leader) to be equidistant from the center of the circle, which I envision as the text itself. This way of being in community is similar to that described in 1 Corinthians 12, where Paul says that the Spirit (the felt presence of God) gives to each person a unique gift and that each of these special gifts is needed for the whole community to function. The community is like a body, where each part is equally important. In this community, one part does not evaluate (put down) either herself (or himself) or evaluate another. Rather, all parts of the body contribute unique gifts to the functioning of the whole, and all parts are to listen for direction, not to one another (How can a hand tell an eye what to do?) but to the coordinating center of the whole community (body)—the Holy Spirit.

It is important for the leader and the group to keep this basic model in mind. It implies that the leader has one among many equally valuable functions. It implies that the overall responsibility for the group lies in the Spirit. This does not mean that all contributions are inspired or direct revelation from God. The issue is rather who is responsible for the group. The leader needs to be responsible *to* the group; all participants including the leader are responsible to God; but God is responsible *for* the group—including the leader. The leader is the one who sets the ground rules, who asks the questions, who determines the overall pace, who may have some information others do not have and need to have, and who sets up the rest of the steps of the method. But this is just one valuable function carried out in the group. The leader in this method does not claim to be *the* expert, the leader does not set up tests and give out grades. Nor is the leader in this method a facilitator (as in a therapy group) of encounter between group members. The leader in this method carries out a unique role that can be only partly described on paper. The best way to learn it is to be in a group first as a participant and to try it with feedback (on your skill as a leader) from a leader with experience in this method.

I'd now like to describe the method itself, with emphasis on what leaders need to do and know. In Chapters V through VIII, there are leaders' guides for four sequences of texts. Each is designed for a weekend retreat with five blocks of time for programming, or one program time-slot on five successive days, or once a week over a five-week period. In the retreat format, I have spread them out over two years of fall and spring retreats, but they could also be used as a one-year series of adult/older youth retreats or for a group that met for twenty weeks throughout the year on a given evening for two to three hours each night.

The most important thing a leader needs is to be personally committed to moving toward wholeness. This way of working with scripture is difficult without a commitment to growing yourself. I do not mean that one has to be especially "religious" or whatever. Rather, the leader needs to have and convey that he or she is excited about working with scripture in this way, that he or she expects new pieces of truth to emerge out of this process each time, and that he or she is open to being personally and deeply challenged to grow each time a group gathers around the scripture in this way.

First let's review all the steps of this method before describing each step in detail.

STEP 1   *Active Listening.* Getting inside the text on its own terms. The leader's task is to share the questions that emerge from the text. The group's task is to use its creative imagination to come up with as many hunches as possible in response to the questions.

STEP 2   *Bridge-building.* Building a bridge (in silence) from the text to one's hidden dimensions, so that the person (piece) in the text can walk across, find, and call forth the "twin" in each person. Building a bridge from the hidden dimensions out into the world (by speaking).

STEP 3   *Identifying Learnings.* Writing down what each person learned about (or for) himself or herself from Steps 1 and 2.

STEP 4   *Identifying Wants.* Given the learnings in Step 3, what does each person want to do (not what he or she *should* do)?

STEP 5   *Goal-setting.* Transforming the want statement into a short-term behavioral goal.

STEP 6   *Covenanting.* Public commitment to the goal and to sharing results with others.

STEP 7   *Sharing How It Went.* Carrying out the covenant stated in Step 6.

The first task of a leader is to search for the questions that arise out of the text itself. The best resource one can bring to this task is a vivid sense of curiosity. It is almost as if we need to be like children who watch an adult do something they have not seen done before, children who ask about everything and anything. This is the most important resource we have, and I recommend using it before consulting any other resources (including the suggestions in Chapters V through VIII). We need to develop and nurture our own brand of inquisitiveness; turning too soon to the product of the inquisitiveness of others can hinder, rather than promote, this development. Also, the questions we develop need to be *ours*, even if we use those others have developed. If the leader feels confident about the questions she or he uses, it has a positive contagious effect on the group.

A second step is to use the diagram of human interaction we've been looking at to help you develop your own questions. You will probably have more questions than could possibly be used in any given group time—and that is good. You can select from the questions the ones that seem most crucial for moving people through the text. And it is helpful to have some questions in reserve. Let's take one example from a story we have already touched on, the healing of Bartimaeus (Mark 10:46–52). Mark 10:47 reads: "And hearing that it was Jesus of Nazareth, he began to shout (and say): 'Son of David, Jesus, have mercy on me!'" The above words are what we sense. So far, we are still within the dotted lines of the diagram. (See Figure 1.)

Some sample questions that would remain within the dotted lines would be (just to establish that we have all "sensed" the same thing):

- What did Bartimaeus actually hear?*
- What did he not hear?
- What did he add to what he heard?
- What does the text say about his volume level?
- What did he actually shout?
- What did he not shout (say)?*

---

*These two questions are more speculative, but they establish that we always select something out of the available options to say and they

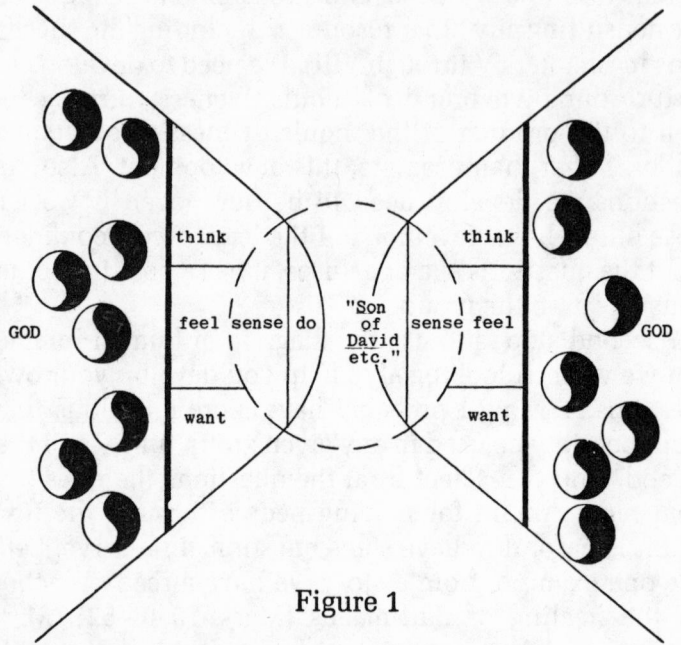

Figure 1

Some sample questions from the three hidden conscious dimensions—thinking, feeling, wanting—would be:

- When Bartimaeus heard that it was Jesus, what might he have thought? felt? wanted?
- Why did he shout?
- Why not ask someone to go to Jesus for him?
- When Jesus heard Bartimaeus' words, what might he have thought? felt? wanted?
- Why does Bartimaeus call Jesus "Son of David"?
- Who else are sons of David?
- When he shouted "Have mercy on me," what did Bartimaeus want?

might establish that he did not say what we thought (think) he said. When I wrote a first draft of this material, I put in that he said, "Lord, have mercy." He did *not* say "Lord" in the Markan version. Matthew *adds* the word Lord. I remembered it from there and unconsciously projected it into the Markan text.

There are many plausible answers, including money ("Have mercy on me" was an expression used by beggars), attention, forgiveness, restoration of sight.

- What did he think Jesus would do?

Some sample questions from the unconscious dimension (behind the bold vertical lines):

- What were the attitudes toward blindness in Jesus' day (or in our day, for that matter)?
- What would Bartimaeus have to think/believe about himself/others/God to do what he did?
- How might he have come to these beliefs?
- What function did blind beggars serve for others?
- If a blind person were to regain his or her sight (and presumably no longer need to beg), how might that seem to affect sighted people negatively?
- Why might a blind person not want to regain his or her sight?
- What are the risks/challenges in becoming sighted (again in this case)?
- What role do deviants play in society in general?
- What do deviants do for the nondeviants?

As you can see, many questions are in the text just waiting to emerge under the right conditions. And this is not an exhaustive list. Even though I have led people through this passage, using this method, many times, new questions emerged as I wrote this.

It is important to learn as much as possible about the physical setting (Jericho, in the case of Bartimaeus) of a passage and to look at the passages that precede and follow the one you are dealing with, to see where the Gospel writer sets the story. If the story is in all three Gospels, is the setting different, and if so, why? For example, why does Mark have the Bartimaeus story on the way out of Jericho, and Luke on the way in? It is also important to learn as much as possible about the cultural-religious assumptions of the day, especially those that come into play in the passage you are examining. In Jesus' day, blindness was thought to be God's punishment for sin. Thus the disciples' first thought when they saw another blind person was to ask Jesus, "Rabbi, who sinned, this man or his parents? [John 9:2 NEB]."* Another important concern, especially when dealing with the Gospels, is the formation of those narratives. How did they come into being? With this information as background, more questions will emerge.

Information regarding the setting can be obtained through a resource like the *Interpreter's Dictionary of the Bible*. There are other resources, but this is one of the best in English that is readily available. The same source can provide valuable information about the cultural and religious assumptions on such issues as blindness. The Bible itself is a gold mine in this area. Cross-references can be found in a resource like the Oxford Study Bibles or in a concordance. The whole ninth chapter of John, for example, shows so much about what the attitudes were toward blindness and how these attitudes affected people's behavior.

Most of the standard textbooks on the Old and New Testaments contain information on the formation of the Gospel narratives. The history of the formation and the basic pattern in the Synoptic Gospels† (Matthew, Mark, and Luke) is important for most of the texts we will be

---

*There was some speculation among the rabbis as to whether a fetus could sin in the womb.

†The word synoptic comes from a Greek word that means "to see together." We owe the expression Synoptic Gospels to J.J. Griesbach, who was the first to split off the Gospel of John and print the Gospels of Matthew, Mark, and Luke in parallel columns, so that they could be seen together and their interrelationship studied. His book *(Synopse der Evangelien des Matthäus, Markus und Lukas)* was published, ironically, in 1776, and it played a crucial part in the New Testament scholarship's movement to independence.

looking at in Chapters V through VIII. While this information is supposed to be common knowledge, most laypeople are either unfamiliar with it or have forgotten it.

The first step in the Gospel formation is the initial events. At this level it is important to realize that there is nothing that "just happened." As soon as something happens, it gets filtered through the interpretive process of those involved, and what the people see and hear is influenced by the unconscious dimensions we have mentioned. Even if one is present and watching, it is difficult to observe well enough to be able to report what actually happened. My children used to ask me to intervene in their quarrels and to blame the one who started it (always the other one). But even if I was observing intently, it was often difficult to tell who started it. I eventually stopped trying altogether. So the first step in the formation of the Gospels is richly complex human interaction.

The reports of these initial events were passed on orally for a period of about thirty years. Once again, we are looking at an interactive process—this time between the stories and those reporting them. It is important to underline the plural (stories) here. Most of the stories, parables, and so on, circulated as independent units, and each of them has a history. In this process, some things changed more than others. Overall, the stories were passed on with far more fidelity to the original than we might expect, because people in that day were used to remembering and reporting oral material more than we are today. If they wanted to remember something, they did not jot it down, they memorized it. Writing was a special profession. Even an educated person like Paul dictated his letters.

The next step was gathering some of the stories together. The passion narratives may have been gathered together earliest, and then collections of sayings or teachings of Jesus. The next step was the writing of the Gospels themselves. Once again the stories were not "just reported"; they were filtered through the belief systems of the writers. There was also some editing and revising done after the Gospels were written.

It is important to realize that we do not have in the Gospels simple, factual accounts. Actually, we never have an objective account of *any* historical event. In fact, all we can have is an "objectifying" account, one that reflects the subjective belief that the things which can be objectively reported are the most important ones to relate. All in all, however, we have a remarkably accurate account in the Gospels. The very fact that we have four different Gospels, each of which gives its own description of the same events (plus several noncanonical gospels), gives us a unique and unusually reliable base with which to work. The fact that the Gospel writers did not attempt to create one harmonious account with no internal contradictions inspires confidence. (They seem to have ascribed to a Mode IV approach to truth.)

The interrelationship of the three Synoptic Gospels looks something like Figure 2. There is much debate about the actual dates, but there is general agreement about the basic interrelationship of the Gospels. Mark is assumed to have been the first Gospel written. Matthew and Luke probably had Mark in front of them as they

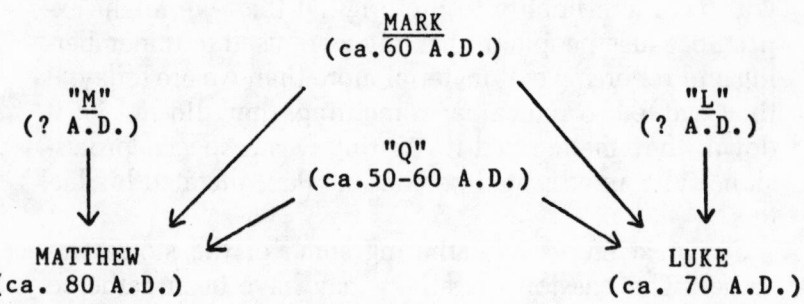

Figure 2

wrote their Gospels. In addition, Matthew and Luke had a source that we call "Q" (from the German word *Quelle*, source), which contained mostly teachings of Jesus. In addition, Matthew had some special material ("M")—things like his birth narrative. And Luke had some special material (which we call "L")—for example, the parable of the compassionate Samaritan. As we track the process from Mark to Matthew and Luke, we can see how they sought to make these stories relevant to their readers or listeners, and we can get some valuable clues for ourselves as we seek to do the same thing.

Because we have several Gospels, we can track what happened to the stories about Jesus as they evolved through the years, and we can attempt to reverse that process in order to get back to Jesus himself. As we do this, we need to remember that it is difficult to establish whether he actually said or did any one thing. Scholars differ on what they accept as "authentic," according to the approach each one uses. But we can look at the flow of the tradition and use our creative imaginations to try to reverse that process. As we do this, we are in a sense following in the footsteps of the Gospel writers themselves, for the Gospels were written to preserve the legacy and reality of the human being Jesus of Nazareth. One example of what happened in the tradition about Jesus is the account of his baptism, which we cover in detail in Chapter V. The synoptic account and the other references to this event are found in paragraph six of the *Gospel Parallels* (hereafter referred to as G.P.).[1]

In Figure 3 the "videotape line" refers to what would have happened if we had been able to make a videotape of the events in Jesus' life, including the voiced* thoughts, feelings, and wants of the people involved. The top line

---

*We need to remember that much is not audible or visible even if one has a camera and tape recorder preserving (a part) of what is happening at any given moment.

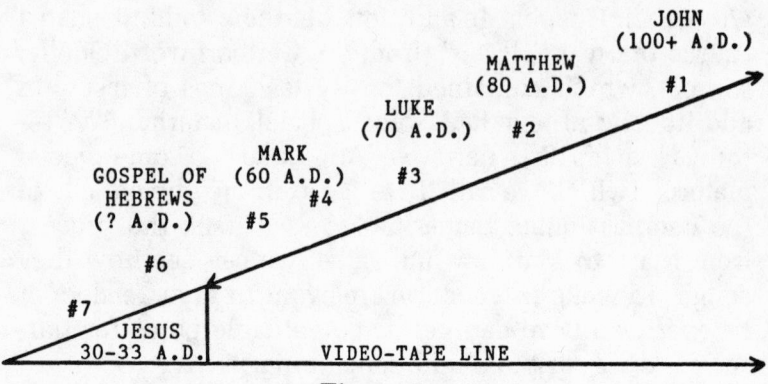

Figure 3

shows what often occurred in the flow of the tradition—
the further out in time you go, the farther away you get
from the bottom line. In the example of baptism, a thorny
issue for the early church was why Jesus was baptized,
since John's baptism was a "baptism of repentance for the
forgiveness of sins [Mark 1:4, RSV]." (See Figure 3, #5.) A
Jesus, who, like other people, would come to John the
Baptist in need of repentance and having sinned was not
in accord with an exalted view of Jesus. Such an act
would have made him subordinate to John and too human. The Gospels wrestled with this in differing ways. In
the Gospel of John, the baptism itself almost disappears,
and John the Baptist recognizes Jesus as "the Lamb of
God" from afar (John 1:29ff.); see Figure 3, #1. In Matthew 3:14, John tries to keep Jesus from being baptized
and says, "I need to be baptized by you [RSV]"; see Figure
3, #2. But Jesus persuades John to go ahead with it. In
Luke, Jesus seems to be baptized almost by accident
"when all the people were baptized" (Luke 3:21, RSV); see
Figure 3, #3. In Mark, Jesus comes and is straightfor-
wardly baptized by John (Mark 1:9); see Figure 3, #4. In
the Gospel According to the Hebrews, there is a conversation between Jesus and his family prior to his going, and
his brothers say, "John the Baptist baptizes for the for-

giveness of sins; let us go and be baptized by him." But Jesus said to them, "In what have I sinned that I should go and be baptized by him? Unless, perhaps, what I have just said is a sin of ignorance."[2] (See Figure 3, #6.) This last passage from the Gospel According to the Hebrews provides an interesting clue to what was on people's minds and may provide a bridge to the meaning of the baptism for Jesus himself. We can at least ask the question "Given the flow of the tradition, what might this event have meant to Jesus himself?" (See Figure 3, #7.) And what we have done with this event can be done with other passages about Jesus as well.*

Assuming that all the homework has been done and the list of questions is ready, the next step for a leader is to spend some time going over the questions before the group meets. It is also helpful to set everything aside for a while and spend some silent, alone time. The purpose of this time is to get centered, to envision the text as your personal center, just as it will, it is hoped, become the center of the group. The last step is to entrust the whole process to God. As a leader, you are not alone in this.

When the group has gathered, begin only when people are in a circle. I have tried to proceed with one or two sitting back from the circle and it does not work. The next step is to go around the group and have people share their names and maybe one personal thing about themselves. I sometimes do some "group-building" beyond this, but that seems to just happen as you go along. After that, I say a *few* words about the method and some of its basic assumptions. The crucial part of this is to go over—and post somewhere—the basic ground rules. For Step 1 (actively listening to the text), the ground rules I use are:

---

*It is important to be aware that the later Gospels may contain more primitive material. One simply needs to develop a feel for the general development of the tradition and go from there.

1. All ideas are OK.
2. No evaluation of self or others.
3. No right or wrong answers (except when establishing the context of the text, or with questions of actual information such as places).
4. Listen for and respect the hunches that emerge out of your own deepest places; set aside your internal critic.
5. Be curious and playful.
6. No debate.

The ground rules for Step 2 (bridge-building) are the same as above, with the addition of:

1. Any member may pass during any sharing, or share as much or as little as he or she wishes.
2. No feedback on things shared during this step.
3. Silence (except in a role-play).
4. The private work of others is to be respected.
5. Confidentiality; things shared here stay here, unless sharer gives permission otherwise.

The stating and posting of these ground rules saves the leader and the group time and energy. If they are not put out up front, they have to be hammered out as you go along. I prefer to have them at the beginning.

The above steps are only taken one time, although you may need to refer to the ground rules now and then. But each time you start a new session together, it is good to spend some time in group silence, during which all are encouraged to be open to the leading of the Spirit and to allow the text to become the center of the group. (Prayer or guided meditation may also be used as a way of getting centered.) Before going into the details of the text, the whole text should be read out loud by one or more people, while the others follow along. Each participant needs a Bible and, for the Synoptic Gospels, a Gospel parallels using the *Revised Standard Version*, such as the one edited by Burton Throckmorton Jr. and published by Thomas Nelson.[3]

Some other preliminary steps may be called for. If it is a group's first time with the Synoptic Gospels, some basic information about the interrelationship of the three is useful. Also, depending on the makeup of the group, it may be important to go over some of the issues raised in Chapters II and III—styles of communication, use of questions, the humanness of Jesus—and the diagram of human interaction. I cannot say exactly when to put in these optional pieces, but it is important to keep the opening presentations as brief as possible. In general, groups of all laypeople or all clergy can move quickly into this process, while groups of laity and clergy together sometimes have a harder time. The difficulty of the clergy-laity "mix" seems to arise from the need of clergy to be seen as authorities and the need of the laity to see clergy that way as well. When you have this mix, you may have to pay special attention to the ground rules.

Once you start, simply ask your first question. Then push for as many hunches as possible. Usually there are one or two and then a pause. At this point, do not answer your own question. That's a mistake, because you'll get trapped into the role of an expert and the group will stop working. Simply restate the question and ask for more hunches. After you've got another, ask "What else?" When you've gotten a number of hunches, move on to the next question. At the beginning stages you may have to reassure the group that you are not asking for more hunches because the first ones were not good enough. It is also best not to evaluate any hunches as "good" or whatever. You, as leader, need to model the ground rules.

Once in a while you may get a question from the group. If you want to deal with it, fine, but do not answer it yourself. Turn to the group and restate it for them. If you don't want to deal with it, say, "I will be glad to talk to you about it after the group is over." The one exception is a question of fact. If no one knows where Jericho is and you do, you may want to share that. Or if you know of a cross-reference that might help, share where it is, but let someone else look it up and read it to the group. Sometimes a group member will want to jump ahead in the text. This is usually not helpful. Simply acknowledge the person and assure him or her that you will get to it. But if you do this, make sure you *do* get to it. Above all, remember that the goal of this step is to get inside the text so that it becomes a living, breathing reality. This will happen. Be patient; trust your questions. You do not have to be an expert to lead this style. But you *are* the leader.

Once you've completed Step 1 you are ready for Step 2, *Bridge-building*. When you are leading a group, it is important to reserve time for Step 2 and for Step 3. Without Step 2, the potential transformative energy created in the first step will dissipate. If the group is meeting weekly, it helps to complete *all* the steps in each session. If the group is meeting over a weekend, or in some similar setting, Steps 4 through 6 may be held until the final session. In this case, if each participant keeps a diary or record of each session, the material for doing Steps 4 through 6 will be at hand for the last session.

The purpose of Step 2 is to identify those pieces in ourselves which correspond to the pieces or people in the text. This is a bit like reversing the process of projection described earlier. Whereas the person who is projecting says, "I am glad I am not like that _____," in this step we intentionally seek to find out how we *are* like the various pieces or parts of a text. The best way to try this out is to look around the room you are in right now and focus on something. Now create a statement that goes like this: "I am like the _____ (what you focused on) in that I. . . ." The thing I focused on just now was a roll of cellophane tape. The statement that popped into my mind was "I am like the cellophane tape in that I try to patch together pieces (people) that have been torn apart." There is a timely truth to that, as often happens, and it is not entirely comfortable at the moment.

This is one of the bridging techniques I use. It involves taking the various pieces or people in the text and writing out a series of statements (in silence). It is important to include all the people or groups involved, because the ones you, as a leader, leave out might be the very ones that some people in the group need to deal with the most. In the Bartimaeus text, this would involve at least the statements "I am like Jesus (in this particular text) in that I . . ."; "like Bartimaeus in that I . . ."; "like Jesus' companions in that I . . ."; and "like the crowd or bystanders in that I. . . ." I speak of pieces of a text because some of the key parts of a text may be objects. I recall one person who went beyond what I asked in response to the text where the woman anoints Jesus' feet. He finished for himself, in addition to the ones I suggested, a sentence that said "I am like the alabaster flask of ointment in that. . . ." The key element in the statement that followed was his response to her breaking open the jar to be able to release its contents. Somehow that act triggered something in him that started him down (or up) a long path away from the things that had been holding him in bondage. This small piece launched him on a new and significant movement toward wholeness.

Another useful bridging technique is art. I always have a variety of different media available: chalk, crayons, cray-pas, watercolors, markers, colored pencils, and so on. I also have materials to make collages, as well as Play-Doh, finger paints, and a variety of other things that can be utilized by nonsighted as well as sighted people. I rarely specify the media to be used, because I want people to feel free to experiment and because I want to include nonsighted people. The purpose or goal of using artwork is the same as the first bridging technique—to allow the pieces or people in me that correspond to the pieces or people in the text to come to consciousness. The important thing to stress in using these media is the purpose. The purpose is *not* to create things that might get an "A" from an art teacher. To get into this, we must leave behind the critic inside us that says, "That's no good, crumple it up and throw it away." All pictures, all creations are OK, just as all ideas are OK. The main point is to use these media to allow our conscious parts to emerge. Art is so suited to this, for so many of us, because it requires no words (which often block the voice of the unconscious). I have personally had a history of being depressed about my artistic ability, but I enter into this artwork with great zest now because I know what it is for and what healing insights it has helped me achieve. As Jung said, "To paint what we see before us is a different art from painting what we see within."[4]

Another medium I use is silent dialogue, which I first learned from Ira Progoff in a workshop (he has since written about it in a book[5]). This involves taking the main people in a passage, writing their names on a piece of paper along with your own, and allowing each person to speak (on the paper) from his or her perspective about an issue. To make this work, silence is crucial (as in other bridging techniques). It helps to sit in as relaxed a position as possible, preferably in a chair with both feet on the floor, and to spend some time doing some deep, slow breathing with eyes closed at first. Once this is done, you just start with one of the people you have chosen "saying" something and allowing the others to "speak" in the order that seems to just happen. Some words of caution are in order. Like the other techniques, it can be very powerful. I have learned some mind-boggling things through the use of dialogue, but some people have a difficult time using this medium. As a leader, you should be aware of this and be available for people to talk privately about it afterward. As with all the other bridging techniques, I would not ask others to do this unless I had done it myself and was willing to do it along with others each time.

Another useful technique is mime. Like dialogue, I would not recommend that mime be used in the first or second session. For mime to work well, people must have built up a sense of trust in the group and have had some experience with the way of being together that characterizes this method—the sense of continuing to be a separate individual within a community, the sense that the group respects the privacy of each individual even while the group is together.* For mime to work, each person needs to stay focused on what he or she is doing. It is very tempting and counterproductive to mentally wander away and worry about what others are doing or what others might think about you. It is sometimes easier to do the miming with eyes closed or half closed. To get into the mime, the group needs to spread out as much as possible within a space where all can hear the leader. The leader then talks the group through the text, with each person in the group physically acting out, in turn, all the roles in the text, without speaking.

There are other techniques, such as role-play,[6] but the main thing to remember is the purpose—to build a bridge from the text to our own hidden dimensions, across which the various people (pieces) in the text can walk and invite their "twins" in us to come out into the light of consciousness. It is also vital that the technique or medium chosen be appropriate to the text; if the chosen technique does not fit well, participants will struggle with it.

---

*I like the image from Gibran's *The Prophet* (New York: Knopf, 1958) in the last part of the section on marriage, which shows this way of being together.

If the bridging technique fits, it can be productive and illuminating. This step can also be quite emotionally powerful for people if they really get into it. It can draw out painful feelings and insights from people's lives, but that is OK and can be very freeing. In my experience, people will go as deep as they are ready for, so a leader should simply give people "space" to react as they want. In this process, the responsibility for what happens is shared by the Holy Spirit. Some people may resist this step; they may say they do not "get it," for example. This usually means that they do not want to "get it" or are not ready for it. The leader's response would be to encourage such people to try it or try something else that will help them identify with the elements of the passage. It is important that those who do not participate in this step respect the privacy of those who do, and that they maintain the ground rule of silence. Respectful silence is so important because this step is aimed at the hidden dimensions of ourselves. Speech draws us away from those dimensions and dilutes the energy needed to break through to them. The only bridging technique I use where speaking is involved is role-play. When role-play is used, however, it needs to be followed by group silence and some means for each person to write or draw the most important parts of the role-play.

At the conclusion of this part of Step 2, the group members return to the circle and share their pictures or writings with the whole group. Remind the participants that they may pass if they choose, that they are to share only what they want to share. If the group is large, the sharing can be done in dyads or triads, or groups of seven to ten people with a facilitator in each group. The facilitator's task is to ensure that no one person dominates and to remind people of the ground rules. These sharing groups could then be used several times throughout the series of sessions. The purpose of this sharing is to give each person the opportunity to verbalize, in a supportive setting, what she or he has done. This builds a second bridge— this time from the hidden dimensions of each person out into the world. The purpose of this is not to elicit feedback from others—that is specifically out of bounds. Feedback is problematic in this kind of setting because it is usually a projection. What we are looking at is a kind of energy conservation. We each need to build up a certain amount of energy in order to deal with changes that we may be called on individually to make. The give-and-take of feedback, with the danger of unrecognized projections, and the defensiveness these projections call forth in others, drains away that energy. This is not an encounter group. The sharing time is still within the model of the individual in community.

Once Step 2 is finished, the challenge still ahead of us is to harness the energy generated so far so that it can have an impact not just on our hidden conscious dimensions but also on our behavior. The tree needs to bear fruit (Matthew 7:20). In a weekend retreat or similar setting, I usually go through at least Step 3 in each session, but I may put a hold on Steps 4 through 6 until the concluding session of the event. (Step 7 is also set up in that concluding session.) If this is the case, the participants should keep some kind of diary or journal as they go along, to record the results of this step for each session. Step 3, *Identifying Learnings*, simply involves writing down what you have learned about or for *yourself* from the interaction of the first two steps. This can be a series of "I learned about (or for) *myself* that . . ." statements. It can also be varied with statements like "I was surprised that I . . ." or "I was disappointed that I. . . ." But the main purpose of this step is to write down whatever insights into yourself have come from Steps 1 and 2.

Step 4, *Identifying Wants*, involves taking a look at the "I learned . . ." statements and translating them into "I want . . ." statements. These are not "I ought to . . ." or "I should . . ." statements. "Oughts" and "shoulds" are simply not a strong enough energy source to enable us to take the risk of moving out into the territory of actually changing our behavior. This step simply involves the completion of the statement "Having learned _____ about myself, I want to. . . ."

Becoming clear about what we *want* to *do* about what we have learned is an important step, but it is not enough to move most of us into new behavior. Most of us have wanted to do many things, but have not done them. It is only when we move from wanting to do something, to deciding what that something will look like, to deciding that we are in fact going to do it that we begin to move into new behaviors. The first part of this process is Step 5, *Goal-setting*—setting a short-term behavioral goal (less than a week). The short-term goal is not intended to implement everything contained in the want statement; it is only meant as a start. The criteria for a short-term goal are:

1. The goal must be *measurable*. It must be possible to do it within a given time frame (preferably less than one week).
2. The goal must be *desirable*. It must be flowing from my "want" energy, not from my "shoulds" or "oughts" (a check to make sure Step 4 was a real *want*).
3. The goal must be *conceivable*. It must be possible to write it down in a few words (no more than two short sentences) in a way that would make sense to someone else as well.
4. The goal must be *believable*. Not only must it make sense to me, but I have to really believe I can do it.
5. The goal must be *do-able*. It has to be actual see-able do-able behavior. A goal such as "I will be

more loving toward my friend" would not be doable behavior; it has to be more concrete. What specific *action* will I take to show how I will be "more loving"?

6. The goal must be *achievable*. The goal has to be within my power to achieve. I might set a goal to run a four-minute mile in the next week but, given my abilities, I know I could not achieve it.
7. The goal must be *controllable*. I might set a goal to take my friend out to dinner this week, but that is not within my control, because it is subject to his or her saying yes. A controllable goal would be to *invite* my friend.
8. The goal must be stated with *no alternative*. "Either/ors" tend to become "neither/nors."
9. The goal must be in accord with my overall value system and be growth-facilitating for me and anyone else involved.

Using these criteria, write the following on a piece of paper:

A goal to be accomplished by _____
(date, time)

I will _____
(Signed) _____

With the completion of Step 5, we have a private commitment to future action. In order to firm up and support that commitment, there are two more steps. Step 6 involves *Covenanting*. Once each person has completed a goal statement, everyone should pair up with one other participant. The first thing they are to do is look over each other's goals to see whether they are indeed conceivable and check them against all the other criteria. Then each pair sets a time (less than a week) and a procedure for checking back with each other to report how it went and what each learned as they worked on their respective goals. In a weekend retreat, the goal-setting (Step 5) and the covenanting are done only in the final session. If a group is meeting once a week, and is going to reconvene in a week's time, this step can be expanded so that each person reads his or her goal to the group as a whole.

The last step, Step 7, *Sharing How It Went,* involves carrying out the covenant entered into in Step 6. If this is a group that will reconvene, the next week's session can begin with each person reporting to the group how it went before going on to the next Step 1.

There is a risk involved in setting a goal and publicly committing oneself to it. But not achieving that goal does not mean failure; it merely means that we have something else to learn, something we had not anticipated when we set the goal. This is really a no-lose process, because the purpose of setting a goal is to help each person on his or her personal journey. Not achieving the goal may be disappointing, but the process of setting it and attempting to achieve it is growth-enhancing in itself.

CHAPTER V

First Sequence:
"What Do You Want Me
to Do for You?"
(Mark 10:51, RSV)

Everything is gestation and then bringing forth . . . let each germ of a feeling come to completion wholly in itself, in the dark, in the inexpressible, the unconscious, beyond the reach of one's own intelligence, and await with deep humility and patience the birth-hour of clarity.

—Ranier Maria Rilke[1]

We get wise by asking questions, and even if these are not answered, we get wise, for a well-packed question carries its own answer on its back as a snail carries its shell.

—James Stephens[2]

Our normal waking consciousness, rational consciousness as we call it, is but one special type of consciousness, whilst all about it, parted from it by the filmiest of screens, there lie potential forms of consciousness entirely different. We may go through life without suspecting their existence; but apply the requisite stimulus, and at a touch they are there in all their completeness.

—William James[3]

The most beautiful and most profound emotion we can experience is the sensation of the mystical. It is the sower of all science. [The one] to whom this emotion is a stranger, who can no longer wonder and stand rapt in awe, is as good as dead. To know what is impenetrable to us really exists, manifesting itself as the highest wisdom and the most radiant beauty which our dull faculties can comprehend only in their most primitive forms—this knowledge, this feeling is at the center of religiousness.

—Albert Einstein[4]

"And why do you pray, Moche?" I asked him. "I pray to the God within me that God will give me the strength to ask . . . the right questions."

—Elie Weisel[5]

These quotations are examples of the ones I put on posters in the room where we hold our sessions. These particular quotations are meant for the first sequence of texts, which begins with the baptism of Jesus. This first sequence is meant to focus both on the beginnings of Jesus' journey and on the issue of the "wanting" dimension of ourselves as the energy source for a change in our lives. Each sample sequence in this book will open with a similar series of quotations, which are also meant as aids in focusing on the issues of the particular sequence of texts involved. These kinds of quotations on posters, along with some selected posters that are commercially available, help make the space special and stimulate reflection between sessions.

As I put together the four sequences of texts, my goal was to track Jesus' "becoming" from his baptism through the resurrection, to the extent that is possible. Much of Jesus' life and ministry could not be covered in the format of four sequences of five sessions each, but many of the key issues of Jesus' life are touched. As I went along, however, a pattern emerged that I had not anticipated. This will not necessarily happen for others, but I want to share what that looked like for me.

The pattern emerged for me first out of Jesus' baptism by John and Jesus' temptations in the wilderness. The more I worked my way into the baptism narrative as presented by Mark, the more it seemed to take on the character of a birth story culminating in Jesus emerging from the "womb" of the water like a newborn child receiving a new set of parents (God and the Spirit). The temptation narrative seemed to be the embodiment of what happens after such a birthing experience—what the "Child" in Jesus received, the "Adult" had to work out. (*If* you are indeed the Child of God, then . . .). The same pattern seemed to emerge in the text in Mark, where Jesus says: "Whoever does not receive the Kingdom of God as a child will certainly not enter it [Mark 10:15]." Once again, the "whoever" that "enters" seems to refer to the decision-making, processing, acting center of ourselves, whether we call that the adult in us or our ego or whatever. But to have something to process, we first have to get in touch with the Child in us, which seems to represent a variety of things—for example, our receptivity to the new, our feelings, our "wants" as opposed to our "shoulds" and "oughts," our potential. I'll be saying more about the "Child" in the next chapter. Although each sequence stands on its own, the first two sequences are aimed more specifically at the "Child." The first sequence targets the "want" dimension of ourselves (a part of the Child) and the second sequence focuses more fully on the Child as a source of healing and as that within us that needs healing. The third and fourth sequences—"Deepening Our Spiritual Journey" and "Getting at the Christian Story Inside Us"—help give direction and focus to the energy generated by the first two.

Each sequence is broken down into five sessions. The first session contains introductory material, which should be used selectively, depending on your personal style of leadership and the needs of the particular group. The first session also has some material to help the group get on board with one another, and some introduction to the theme. This material should also be used selectively. When we come to the texts, there are three kinds of things I'll be sharing: the questions themselves, to serve as *suggestions* of what can be asked; background information for leaders, to be shared with participants when appropriate; occasional comments on translation, when important for understanding the text. The final sessions vary, but I like to end with some kind of worship experience, usually centered around communion in some form. Plans for these worship experiences are finalized only after the fourth session, because they should reflect the experience and needs of each particular group.

In these sessions, the paragraph (¶) numbers given indicate the RSV *Gospel Parallels* (G.P.) published by Thomas Nelson & Sons (1957). But every translation is an interpretation. For example the key Greek word *sodzein* can be translated either "to save" or "to heal." So when Jesus says, "Your faith has *sesoken* you," do you translate that as "healed you" or "saved you" or "made you well" or "made you whole" or something else? One check on the inevitable arbitrariness of translators is to utilize several different translations. The ones I regularly consult in addition to the RSV are the *New English Bible, Today's English Version*, and the *King James Version*.

As part of the introductory session of the first sequence, I deal briefly with the issue of being versus becoming. I begin by inviting the participants to pair off and ask each other a series of questions designed to give them an experiential base for reflecting together on this issue. It would be helpful for you to try it out now also, either with someone else or with an imaginary partner. The first step is to ask each other three times (alternating back and forth) the question, "Who are you?" each time coming up with a different answer. (If you are alone, just complete the sentence "I am . . ." three times with three different things.) The second step is to ask each other back and forth in three rounds, the question "Whom are you becoming?" (If you are alone, just complete the sentence "I am becoming . . ." three times with three different things.) I suspect that the answers to the first series would be things like your name and your roles such as mother, father, teacher, and that the answers to the second series would be processes like "more mature" or "more aware." People asked to compare the two experiences have come up with observations like, "The second was more interesting." "It was more challenging." "We really had to think about the second series." "I learned more about myself from the second." "The first had more to do with the past, the second with the future."

As part of the opening sequence, the next step for the leader would be to say that as we look at the scriptures, we will be looking at and asking questions about issues related mostly to "becoming" rather than "being." As heirs of Western culture, we have been influenced by the legacy of Greek thought, which has led us to take a static view of reality—including ourselves, God, and Jesus. We have tried to define and analyze who we *are*, who God *is*, who Jesus *was*. But these kinds of "being"-related issues were alien to the world in which Jesus lived, influenced as it was primarily by the thought patterns of the Old Testament. The central issues that emerge from this heritage are more ones of "becoming," and the challenge is not to define and analyze who we are, but to ask how we can *become* more fully what we are destined to become, how God responds to or relates to us and to the world as we do that, and how Jesus moved toward the unique destiny that was his.

The primary biblical symbol for the time and place when all life would become what it was destined to become is the kingdom of God. That term, especially in our postmonarchical era, has lost much of its force. When Jesus said, the "kingdom of God is . . . ," that would have had the same kind of here-and-now strength as a modern-day phrase like "The threat of nuclear war is. . . ." So it seems important to search together for some new words that can capture something of what was originally meant by "kingdom of God." For me, one of them has been the term wholeness, which I have seen used more and more. According to Webster, the word whole means, among other things: recovered from a wound; healed; having all its proper parts or components; directed to one end, not scattered or dispersed. "WHOLE implies that nothing has been omitted, ignored, abated, or taken away."⁶ As I said in the Prologue, it goes back to the Old English word *hal*, from which we also get the word healthy. It is related to the German word *Heil* which means both "health" and "salvation."

In the process of moving toward wholeness, the scriptures can be profoundly helpful, especially if we consciously look not for some set of eternal, changeless truths to help us define who we *are*, but rather at the *process*, the movement toward wholeness that we see there to aid us in that same kind of journey. Mark's summary of Jesus' message is an important clue in this. "The right time is now, we don't have to wait for it. The kingdom of God (that realm where everything is put together, where true wholeness is a reality) is near. So repent (begin now to make the changes needed to move toward wholeness), and believe the Good News (we really can do it)." If this is indeed the core of Jesus' message, then by tracking Jesus' own movement toward wholeness from baptism (his birthing process?) through his crucifixion and resurrection (another birthing process?), we can move through a parallel process in our own lives.

Session I. G.P. ¶6, Matthew 3:13–17; Mark 1:9–11; Luke 3:21–22

A. Introduction of participants, with each sharing her or

his name and one thing each person hopes for (wants) out of the time together
B. Overview of what will be covered in the five sessions
C. Options.
   1. Overview of the Diagram of Human Interaction and its significance
   2. Introduction to the Synoptic Gospels
   3. Presentation on the humanness of Jesus
   4. Presentation of the method, with emphasis on the role of questions
D. Presentation of the ground rules
E. Exercise on "being" versus "becoming."
F. The text: The Baptism of Jesus (G.P. ¶6, Matthew 3:13–17; Mark 1:9–11; Luke 3:21–22)

Preparation and Background for Step 1

For this first text, I want to share how I prepare to lead a group through a text. I will give more background information than usual for this text, because it is a crucial starting point for the texts that follow.

The first step in preparation involves reading the text in Mark in its context in the Gospel with a beginner's mind,* as if you knew nothing else about the events that might have come before this as related by other Gospels, and nothing about subsequent events. This is it—Mark is telling you and me a story we have never heard before. As you read Mark 1:1–12, imagine that you will be able to ask Mark anything that comes to mind. You can interrupt him as he goes along, or wait until he finishes. Listen like a child, with a child's curiosity and willingness to risk asking even the most outrageous questions.

---

*Suzuki speaks about the "beginner's mind." "Our 'original mind' . . . is always ready for anything; it is open to everything. In the beginner's mind there are many possibilities; in the expert's mind there are few." Shunryu Suzuki, *Zen Mind, Beginner's Mind* (New York and Tokyo: Weatherhill, 1970), p. 21.

My inner child gets going with John and the desert in verse 4. Who was this John? Where did he come from? What is the desert like? Why go out there? How come he baptized? Where did he get the idea? How can he baptize in a desert? Where did he get the water? My inner child gets "hooked" again with John's clothing and food. Camel's hair—what a strange garment! What did people think? Why did he wear it? What was he trying to do? Did anybody else wear things like that at that time? What about his food? Locusts—yuck! Why would he eat locusts? Wild honey I can see, but locusts? Did other people eat locusts, or was John the only one? What about Jesus? Mark says this is the beginning for him. Who was he? Where was Nazareth? What was Nazareth like? How did he hear about John? How far was it from Nazareth to where John was? How long did it take him? What did he hope would happen? Why did he leave home? What did his family think? Why did Jesus want to be baptized? Did he want to get rid of his sins like all the others? How old was Jesus? Did John know who Jesus was? What was the Jordan River like? Was the river in the middle of a wilderness? Did John push Jesus under the water—or how *did* he do it? The voice from heaven—how did Jesus hear it? Did anyone else hear it? "You are now my son"—what does that mean? Did he like hearing that, or was he afraid? What about his parents—was he no longer their son? If they heard about this, what would they think?

The next step is to focus on the text of the baptism as it appears in Mark 1:9–11 and to fix the details of the text in your mind. Crucial details here are: Jesus' coming alone; the baptism by John (no comment, just done); the Spirit descending like a dove; the voice from heaven saying, "Thou art my beloved Son; with thee I am well pleased [RSV]." Now, using the *Gospel Parallels*, look at the Matthew and Luke texts, asking yourself, What from Mark's account do they keep? What do they add? What do they leave out? What do they change? Why? What might they have been thinking, feeling, wanting, as they did that? What might have influenced them (from behind the bold vertical lines in the diagram, the unconscious dimension)? What might we infer from that about what happened when stories about Jesus were retold?

The third step is to look at the notes that contain textual variants (things that appear in some Greek manuscripts of the New Testament but not in others) and at the related variants from the noncanonical material (things that did not make it into the New Testament as we have it). These give clues to questions people back then were asking and to some of their hunches in response to those questions or vice versa (you may read an "answer" there and have to work back to the question). "Was Jesus baptized for forgiveness of sins?" The hunch of the Gospel According to the Hebrews seems to be, "Sort of." "Is this actually a birthing experience for Jesus?" Several texts say "Yes," by adding the words "Today I have begotten thee" after "Thou art my Son." (These words came from Psalm 2:7—"You are my son; today I have become your father [TEV]"; they appear again in Acts 13:33, where they refer to a second "birthing" experience—the crucifixion and the resurrection). Was this an emotional experience for Jesus, or rather calm? Justin expresses his hunch by saying that when Jesus went into the water, fire was kindled on the Jordan. How old was Jesus? The hunch of the Gospel of the Ebionites is thirty years old.

The next step is to set the whole thing aside for a while. Play with the images, think about your questions. Then go back to Mark and reread that account. Flesh out some of your own personal hunches about the questions that your inner child generated. Take another look at what Matthew and Luke say. Take another look at the variants. What new questions emerge? Don't hurry. A gestation period is necessary. Eventually more questions will emerge, and that is the time to seek information from other sources.

To get started, try a resource like the *Interpreter's Dictionary of the Bible* (IDB).[7] Find out about the places—Nazareth, Galilee, the Jordan River, the wilderness. Find out about the people—in this case, John—and the things mentioned, like water, baptism, Spirit, and dove. Check out John's clothing and food: who else wore camel's hair, and what about the locusts? (For example, you will find that locusts were a "clean" food. They are 75 percent protein, and they are still consumed by desert people today in the area in raw, roasted, cooked, or dried form.)

From this research, you will come across a good deal of information on the Old Testament background. This is important because it gives us clues to the hidden dimensions of people who lived in the first century. It helps us formulate hunches about what they might have been thinking, feeling, and wanting. Jews like John and Jesus were taught the Old Testament from childhood. The IDB often provides excellent references and more than enough information on Old Testament background, but sometimes it is lacking. For example, on the locale of John's ministry, the wilderness, the IDB is brief and not too helpful. In such a case, you can draw on your own memory and you can use a concordance. In what situations has the wilderness seemed important in the Old Testament? Pursue it further by looking up the word wilderness in a concordance and tracking down the references. The IDB again provides little information in the case of camel's hair. It gives two Old Testament references (from 2 Kings 1:8 and Zechariah 13:4), but it does not give a sense of the sequence or what Zechariah 13:4 actually says. Elijah wore this type of garment in the ninth century B.C.E. In the intervening time (many centuries), so many had tried to wear this garment to pretend to be prophets that the prophet Zechariah looks forward (in 13:4) to when no one will wear a garment like this to deceive people. So when John chooses to wear a garment like this in the course of his prophetic task, it says what about John? In other words, with the appropriate background, we still do not have the one right answer, but at least we may have the right question.

The IDB, *Gospel Parallels,* concordances, and various Bible translations are the best tools in general, and they are readily available, but there are many more specialized resources that can be helpful if you have access to them. A basic knowledge of Greek can give you access to the original text (though we must remember that Jesus' native language was probably Aramaic) and with the help of an interlinear translation (i.e., literal English rendering under each Greek word) you can gain important insights. For example, where the RSV and many other translations have in verse 10 "the heavens opened," the Greek is from the verb *schizo,* which means to tear apart or to rend (from which we get the word schizophrenia—"split mind"). The same word is used in Matthew 27:51 to describe the tearing apart of the curtain that hung in front of the innermost part of the temple where God was thought to dwell (or hide?). Such a small detail gives us a feel for the power of this moment in Jesus' life. It is also suggestive in another way: At both "birthing" points in Jesus' life, God is exposed and with this kind of nakedness comes what? God has become what at the first birthing point? At the second birthing point? Once again a significant question emerges out of a wholistic style of research.

Another valuable resource is the German commentary on the New Testament by Herman Strack and Paul Billerbeck,[8] a vast collection of rabbinical material that provides background for various New Testament passages. For example, I was puzzling about the phrase "daily bread" in the Lord's Prayer, and in this source I found several rabbinical stories that went something like this: There was a man who had a son; the father gave his son enough bread for a year; the father did not see him again until the next year; the father then decided to give his son only enough bread for one day at a time; he then saw him every day. This opened up new possibilities for what "daily bread" might mean.

If you have commentaries available to you, this is the best point to refer to them. However, if you have gone through the process I have outlined to this point, you may well already have as much material at your fingertips as many commentaries provide. And this will be magnified many times over when you take your questions into a group. It is truly striking how much wisdom emerges out of groups using this method.

It is important to note that while the Old Testament background provides many significant clues to the world of the New Testament, there were many other influences as well, some of which come already through the Old Testament itself. There is the influence of the religion of the Canaanites, the inhabitants of Palestine prior to the coming of the Hebrews. There were also influences from the religions of Egypt, Greece, and the Fertile Crescent. Relating to baptism, for instance, were a number of ideas from different places: water sprinkled from above was seen as the fertilizing semen of the gods or the cleansing water sent from the gods; water into which one was immersed was seen as representing the womb of a goddess from which one emerged renewed or reborn, or it was the dwelling place of gods. Any of these ideas would have influenced the thought of people about water and baptism in the time of John and Jesus. For example, in the monastery on Patmos, I saw an early portrayal of the baptism of Jesus. In this painting, there was under the water a picture of a small, startled, strange-looking figure, apparently a remnant of the idea that gods dwelt below the surface of the water.

As twentieth-century people, we need to keep in mind such things in order to be able to get inside the lives of first-century Palestinians. In those days, for example, light was a recurring miracle, not something produced at the flick of a switch. And water was scarce, so that the very presence of water had almost magical significance. A large freshwater lake like the Sea of Galilee was amazing amidst such a vast stretch of barren land. Also, we need to remember that the world was seen as a kind of gigantic domed stadium. On the underside of the "roof" were the stars. Above the roof was a huge quantity of water, part of which came down when God opened the "windows" in the roof. And God could always leave those windows open, as in the time of Noah. Under the "floor" of the stadium there was also water—the great deep—so that any surface water came from and was connected to this water.

The point is that whatever we can learn about life in first-century Palestine will help us ask questions that will enable participants to exercise the kind of active imagination it takes to "hear" what any given New Testament text is saying. What Johan Huizinga says of the Middle Ages might serve as a reminder of the imaginary bridge we have to cross to get into centuries-old texts.

The contrast between silence and sound, darkness and light . . . was more strongly marked than it is in our lives. The modern town hardly knows silence or darkness in their purity, nor the effect of a solitary light or a single distant cry.

All things presenting themselves to the mind in violent contrasts and impressive forms lent a tone of excitement and of passion to everyday life and tended to produce that perpetual oscillation between despair and distracted joy, between cruelty and pious tenderness which characterize life in the Middle Ages.[9]

And much of what he says about the Middle Ages is equally true of the first century.

By now, with the information you have, with your own innate curiosity, and with the diagram of human interaction, you should be ready to compile you own list of questions. Try your hand at this each time, before you look at the questions I will be listing, so that my list will not stifle your creativity. The more you practice this, the better you will get at it.

STEP 1. Active Listening: Mark 1:9–11 (and parallels)

After a time of centering, start by having someone read Mark 1:4–6 to set the scene.

1. Focusing on the wilderness part first to set the scene . . .
   - What is a wilderness like?
   - Why would someone intentionally go into the wilderness?
   - What do we hope will happen there that would not happen elsewhere?
   - What is in a wilderness? What is not in a wilderness?
   - How is a wilderness different from a village or town?
   - As a first-century Jewish person, what historical memories would be associated with "wilderness"?

   In the first century, the wilderness was, among other things, the place where unemployed demons were thought to reside as they waited for someone to inhabit next.

2. Focusing on the clothing of John, why might he have chosen it?
   - What might others think of his clothing?
     Have someone read 2 Kings 1:8.
3. What was Elijah like?

- What is there about John that is like Elijah?

  Have someone read Zechariah 13:4.

4. What does this tell us about what happened in the centuries after Elijah?
5. What might John have had to face in appearing as he did?
6. Focusing on John's diet, what are locusts?
   - Why might he have eaten them?
   - What historical memories would be associated with honey?
7. Taking his appearance and diet together, what does this tell us about John?
8. Focusing on John's actions and message, what does it say he did, and what did he actually say?

In the Hebrew tradition there is no real precedent for a "baptism of repentance for forgiveness of sins." There were ritual washings, such as after a menstrual period, to make one ritually clean, but that had nothing to do with sin. And there was, perhaps, proselyte baptism for people converting to Judaism. But John's baptism was different.

9. If there was no real precedent for John's way of baptizing, where did he get it?

   Option: Have someone read Isaiah 1:15–17 and Ezekiel 36:25–29.

10. What might people have been saying about John?
11. Focusing on the water part, what do we associate with water?
    - What do we do with water?
    - When we cannot get water, what happens?
    - What parts of the life cycle are associated with water?
    - What adjectives describe water?
    - What would a first-century Jewish person associate with water?
    - Who in the Old Testament went into or under the water, and under what circumstances?

Option: Read 1 Corinthians 10:1–4.

- All in all, then, water symbolizes what?

    Shifting to the baptism itself, have someone read the Markan narrative from G.P. ¶6, Mark 1:9–11.

12. Recall first what John's baptism was for. It was a baptism of . . . ?

13. Assuming that this is the "beginning" for Jesus, as Mark says (Mark 1:1), and assuming that he was like other people who had heard about who John was and what he was doing, why might Jesus himself have wanted to go to John?
    - What might he have felt as he went?
    - What might he have expected (thought)?
    - What did he have to leave behind to go?
    - What might he have thought about that?
    - What might his feelings have been?

    It is important to bring a beginner's mind to this, to stick with what Mark tells us, and not to anticipate what comes next.

14. Compare what Matthew and Luke do to the account of Mark. What does Luke change? Why?
    - What does Luke leave out? Why?
    - What does he keep?
    - What does Matthew change? Why?
    - What does he add? Why?
    - What do we learn from this about what happened in the tradition to the portrayal of Jesus?

15. Look at the note to Matthew 3:13 from the Gospel According to the Hebrews. What does that add?

16. The note to Mark 1:11 indicates that the words of this verse are taken from Psalm 2:7, and many sources have the whole verse, including the words "Today I have begotten you." What might those who included these words have been thinking about this event?

- What might those who did not include these words have been thinking?
- What is at stake here?

17. Returning to the baptism itself, as Jesus came to John, what might he have been thinking? feeling? wanting?
    - How did John know that Jesus wanted to be baptized?
    - If something seems to be missing here, how did it get left out? Why?
    - What might John have said to Jesus prior to the baptism?
    - How might Jesus have replied?

18. When Jesus was baptized, he probably would have been lowered backward into the murky water of the Jordan River. Imagine for a minute what it feels like to be lowered backward. You might recall dreams of falling backward. What feelings are associated with this?
    - Into what do you feel you are falling?
    - So what might Jesus have been feeling as he went under?

      Remember the question "What else?"
    - What part of our lives do we spend surrounded by water?
    - What resonances might this immersion in water kick off then?

19. Both Matthew and Luke soften the next step in the process. Mark says that when Jesus came out of the water, the heavens immediately ripped open or tore apart, or rent asunder (the verb *schizo*). Matthew and Luke change that to the verb *anoigo*, which simply means "were opened" in this case. If we stick with Mark, what feelings might be evoked by the heavens ripping open?
    - If this were a birthing type of experience, of what

part of the birthing process would it be reminiscent?

20. If you indeed saw the heavens ripping open or being torn apart, and were to imagine some bird emerging out of that opening, what bird might that be?
21. What actually emerges?
22. What effect might that have on someone? It would evoke what kind of response?

In the Old Testament, the Spirit frequently "seizes" or "takes possession of" a person (compare 1 Samuel 10:6, 10; 11:6). We probably have here one of those places where we do not see the impact, even the humor, of a passage, because we do not have the antenna of a first-century person to pick up the full message with all its nuances. There seems to be no Spirit-dove linkage in the Hebrew heritage as such. There is the role of the dove in the Noah flood experience, and that may play some part in this passage. The dove did signal that the flood was over. If that does play into this, it says something about the nature of the experience for Jesus. There is, however, a clear linkage of the dove to the Canaanite mother-goddess Ashera,[10] who was appealed to by mothers in childbirth. In Hebrew, the spirit is feminine in gender, and this is at least suggestive of a part of what might be emerging here.

23. After the Spirit descends like a dove, the text says that a voice came from heaven. Whose voice is this?
    - What are the options?
    - Whose voice might Jesus have thought it was?
    - To whom is the message addressed in Mark? in Matthew?
    - How does Matthew's change alter the experience?
24. With the heavens ripped open like this, what is happening, symbolically at least, to God?
25. Verse 11 says, literally, "You are my son, the loved one, in (with) you I was (am) well pleased." If you were to put that in your own words, what would you say?

26. If this were a birthing type of experience, what in the birth process would this be parallel to?
27. What might Jesus be thinking and feeling as he hears this?

Compare Luke 1:28–29 for Mary's response to a similar message.

28. What happens to Jesus in the baptism?
    - What doesn't happen?
29. What happens to God?
    - How is God now different?
    - What risks did God take?
30. If Jesus is now the son of new parents (God? and Spirit), what does he know about that?
    - What does he not know?
    - What does God know?
    - What does God not know?
31. As he moves away from this experience, what issues are left unresolved?

The above list of questions may seem long, but I wanted to be especially thorough on this first passage to illustrate Step 1 as fully as possible. In practice, I would not ask all these questions.

STEP 2. Bridge-building

Every time the transition from Step 1 to Step 2 is made, it helps to restate the ground rules for Step 2. Because this step involves artwork (if you use my suggestion), you might also say a few words about the purpose of using this medium in this process. I prefer to have the group stay within the same general area in which you have gone through the text for this step. This seems to help preserve the energy generated by Step 1. Because this exercise has three parts, it also enables the leader to reach everybody at once for each phase.

Part A

On a large piece of white paper (at least 12 inches × 18

inches), have the group members use one of the media (e.g., chalk, crayons, finger paint) to paint or draw or sketch the baptism of Jesus. (This helps fix the event in our insides. It also starts the bridging process, because as we draw we connect our insides with the event.)

Then ask the participants to turn the paper over and put a line lengthwise down the middle. On the left side they are to put the word *dying* at the top, and on the right the word *rising*. Invite the participants to put down, in the left column, things in their lives that are dying right now and, in the right column, things that are rising right now.

By way of explanation, each moment of acting represents a choice *to* do one thing and *not* to do something else. To go *to* John, Jesus had to go *away* from home. To take on (rise to) his new role, he had to let go (die to) his old role. So just as his dying and rising at the other end of his life could be seen as a birthing, so this birthing represents a dying and a rising. This is what I am suggesting here—that people identify the pieces in their own lives that are dying or rising right now.

Part B

When everyone is finished, ask people to gather in pairs or small groups or return to the large group to share, in order to verbalize what the experience was like for each person. Remember the ground rules: Each person has the right to pass; when sharing, each person can share as much as he or she wants; what is shared here stays here. The sharing not only helps each person cross back over the bridge, but it also leads naturally to the next step.

STEP 3. Identifying Learnings

Ask each person in the group who wishes to do so to finish the statement "I learned about or for myself. . . ."

STEPS 4–7

Steps 4–7 are described in Chapter IV and are the same each time. In subsequent sessions, the second part of Step 2 and Steps 3–7 stay the same, so I will not go through them each time, even though I hope they will be done each time.* In a weekend retreat, it is usually enough to go through Step 3 in Sessions 1–4, as long as people keep some kind of record to refer to in the final session. For this first sequence, with its focus on wants, I recommend going through Step 4 (Identifying Wants) in each session, so that each participant has a list of wants to use in the final session.

Session II. G.P. ¶8, Matthew 4:1–11; Mark 1:12–13; Luke 4:1–13

Background for Step 1

This story presents some problems for people with the narrow, scientific mind-set that limits reality to the world of tangible objects observable by left-brained methods.[11] But if one assumes that there is always more to reality than any human can observe directly, this story can come alive and help us to gain a fuller understanding of that kind of reality, both "out there" and "within" each of us, and of the deep places where Jesus went and we may need to go on our journey of becoming.

The wilderness referred to in this text is probably the one west of the Jordan River. It is a barren, dry, rugged region of uninviting hills. Having visited this area, and seen this desolate land stretching out in every direction, I had a strong sense of the intensity of Jesus' struggle. This was clearly a *real* experience for Jesus, real enough that

---

*In a weekend retreat, Step 7 is set up in the final session only. If the sessions are done on a weekly schedule, Step 7 is set up at the end of each session.

he later taught people to pray not to be led into this kind of experience.

STEP 1. Active Listening: Mark 1:12–13 (and parallels)

After the participants gather in a circle, and after a time of centering, have someone read Mark 1:12–13.

1. Before going into Mark's account, let us recall first what Jesus had just been through and what questions he took with him from that experience.
2. In the baptism, what might have been the expected action of the Spirit?
   - What happened?
3. Turning to Mark, in verse 12, it says what about the action of the Spirit?
4. What does this suggest about Jesus?
5. Before moving on, I'd like to go back and recall what the wilderness is and what it represents. From the last session then, what do we remember about a wilderness?
   - What historical memories were associated with it?
6. Now add the detail of forty days. What does the number forty kick off as memories from the Old Testament?
7. As the Spirit drove Jesus into the wilderness, he might have been thinking what? feeling what? wanting what?
8. "He was tempted by Satan."

The word translated "tempt" can also be translated "test."

We'll come back to the issue of temptation, but for now I want to focus on Satan. What do we know about Satan?
   - Where in the Old Testament did Satan seem to play a similar role?

9. What is the difference between a wild beast and a tame beast?
   - Wild suggests what qualities?
10. The angels served him or ministered to him. What do we know about angels?
   - How might they have served Jesus?
   - What do angels do elsewhere in the scriptures?
11. If all we had were Mark's account, what might we conclude about Jesus' stay in the wilderness?
   - He was out there doing what?
   - And the experience was like what for Jesus?

Now have someone read Matthew 4:1–11.

12. What is the difference in the action of the Spirit in Matthew 4:1 from Mark 1:12?
   - Which seems more original to you?
   - Why would Matthew change Mark here?
13. Matthew says that Jesus was led by the Spirit in order to be tempted by the devil. What do you make of this linkage between Spirit and devil?
14. In verse 2, Matthew adds two details. What are they?
15. What is fasting?
   - Why do people fast?
   - What happens when you fast that would not happen otherwise?
   - At what point was Jesus hungry?
16. Before going on to the temptations themselves, I want to focus on the issue of temptation itself. What is a temptation?
   - A temptation is addressed to what part of our hidden conscious awareness?
   - What has to happen inside us and outside us for something to be tempting?
   - How does a temptation change when someone else gives voice to that part of us that wants to do what the person is saying?

111

- So in this sequence, what might Jesus be sorting out?
17. In the first temptation (Matthew 4:3), what is the temptation?
    - What good could come if he did this?
    - What would be wrong with it?
    - If Jesus did this, what would people think about him?
    - How would that limit him?
18. Did he never do anything like this?
19. What does Jesus answer?
20. "By everything that *proceeds*"—this is the present tense. What might this signify to Jesus?
21. His answer comes from where?

Have someone read Deuteronomy 8:1–6 out loud.

22. What part of Israel's experience does this come from?
23. Deuteronomy 8:6 speaks of God disciplining as a father disciplines his son; who is doing the disciplining in the wilderness this time?
    - What does this suggest about the God-Satan relationship in this story?
    - About the function of Satan?
    - About the purpose of evil?
24. Does Jesus say no to the temptation?
25. How would saying no or yes have a similar effect on Jesus?
26. In the second temptation (Matthew 4:5–6), what is the temptation?
27. What good could come of it if Jesus did it?
28. Who would likely see this?
29. What is wrong with doing it?
30. Did he ever do something like this?
    - How was what he actually did different?
31. Satan is doing what here?
    - He quotes from where?

- What does that say about quoting scripture?
32. Jesus' answer comes from Deuteronomy 6:16. What is the significance of the answer?

   Option: Have someone read Exodus 17:1–7.

33. In the third temptation (Matthew 4:8), what is the temptation?
34. What good could come from doing it?
35. How could Satan deliver on the promise?
36. The assumption is . . .?
37. Who would see this act as the devil proposes?
38. So all that Jesus would have to do is what?
39. What is wrong with doing this?
40. What in the temptation does Jesus take issue with? What not?
41. Through all this, what has the devil been doing for Jesus?
42. What does Jesus know at the end?
   - What does he not know?
43. What if Jesus had not been driven/led out into the wilderness?
44. How did Jesus handle the temptations?
45. What did he not do? Why?
46. Shifting into Luke, Luke says the devil left only to return later. When was that, and in what form?

STEP 2. Bridge-building

Part A

Any one of several different exercises can be used here. One exercise involves asking the group members to complete the following sentences on a sheet of paper.

I am like Jesus (in this passage) in that I _____.
I am like the Spirit (in this passage) in that I _____.
I am like the devil (in this passage) in that I _____.
I am like the angels (in this passage) in that I _____.

I am like the wild beasts (in this passage) in that I

_____.

I am like the wilderness (in this passage) in that I

_____.

Another option is to ask people to draw/paint/sketch the wilderness experience, including in the picture the part of themselves that is like Jesus, the Spirit, etc.

Then there is an exercise that pulls Sessions I and II together. Participants make a kind of chart of their lives. Each person takes a large piece of paper and draws a line horizontally through the middle. Above the line, each person is to draw *symbols* of his or her peak experiences or birthing moments. Below the line go symbols of any testing experiences that followed those already above the line.

Part B

Part B involves sharing and is the same as described in Part B of Session I (see p. 108).

STEPS 3–7

Steps 3–7 are the same as described in Session I (see pp. 108–9).

Session III. G.P. ¶193, Matthew 20:29–34; Mark 10:46–52; Luke 18:35–43

Background for Step 1

We looked at parts of this text as an example in the previous chapters, so some needed background is already in place. It is especially helpful to read all of John 9, which shows how embedded in the social fabric an issue like blindness is, and what kind of changes must take place in the society for individuals to move toward wholeness. The final verses (39–41) are especially striking. I recommend that participants too read John 9 in preparation for this session. For leaders, I recommend the reading of the IDB articles on alms, blindness, and Jericho.

STEP 1. Active Listening: Mark 10:46–52 (and parallels)

After a time of centering, have one or more participants read the passage Mark 10:46–52.

1. Setting the scene first, what do we know about Jericho?
   - Where is it?
   - What kind of place is it?
2. What was its history?
3. Where is Jesus going?
   - What is behind him?
   - What is ahead for him?
4. What do we know about blindness in the first century?
5. When you see a blind person today, what are your feelings? thoughts? wants?
6. How differently do you act toward a person who is blind?
7. In verse 46, Bartimaeus means "son of Timaeus." Why do you think Mark translates it?
8. How does Luke change this verse?
   - Why might he have made these changes?
   - What is the impact of these changes?
9. How does Matthew change this verse?
   - Why might he have made these changes?
   - What impact does that have?
10. In verse 47, Bartimaeus hears that it is Jesus of Nazareth and begins to cry out. How did he know about Jesus?
    - Why does he cry out, or shout?

The verb *kradzein*—shout—is a forceful word.

   - What else could he have done?
   - Why did he not do that?

11. What does he actually shout?
    - What might he have wanted?
12. Why does he address Jesus as "Son of David"?
    - Who else might have been thought of as a son of David?

"Son" is not capitalized in the Greek.

13. What did Bartimaeus think Jesus might do?
14. Given what we know about blindness in the first century, what would Bartimaeus have had to think about himself to shout in this way?
15. In verse 48, many rebuke him and tell him to be quiet.

The word translated "rebuke" is a harsh word expressing anger and implying a put-down.

    - Why do they do this?
    - What is at stake for them?
    - What if someone shouted like this in a church today?
    - What feelings ... thoughts ... wants ... behaviors ... would be evoked in others?
16. What function do blind beggars play in a society?
17. What function do deviants (those who depart from the norm) play for the normal ones in society?
18. But Bartimaeus does what? Why?
19. Jesus apparently hears (this time?), stops, and says, "Call him!" To whom is Jesus speaking?
    - How might they feel at this point?
    - What does Jesus think now? feel now? want now?
20. Luke changes this verse in what way?
    - What might have influenced Luke to make this change?
    - What impact does the change have?
21. If Mark's version is more original (which is likely), why did Jesus have them "call" Bartimaeus?
22. What does it do for Bartimaeus to be "called" rather than "brought"?

23. Both Matthew and Luke leave out verse 50 of Mark. Why?
24. What does Bartimaeus do in verse 50?
    - What does this tell us about his feelings? thoughts?
25. In verse 51 it actually says Jesus "answered" Bartimaeus. What is he answering or responding to?
26. Jesus' "answer" takes what form?
27. Why does Jesus ask?
    - What does this question do for Bartimaeus?
    - Even if Jesus knew, why would it be important to ask?
    - Jesus is treating Bartimaeus as what?
28. Bartimaeus' response is literally, "Rabbi, that I may see again." What might have influenced the translators to drop the "again" and insert the "let me"?
    - How would you put the sentence into smooth English, that is, what would you insert?
29. What are the implications of Bartimaeus' having once been sighted and then losing his sight (as opposed to having been born blind)?
30. What does Bartimaeus stand to gain by becoming sighted?
    - What do others lose?
    - What are the risks or challenges for Bartimaeus in becoming sighted?
    - What does he lose?
31. Jesus responds to Bartimaeus, literally, "Go. Your faith has healed you (or saved you or made you whole)." What are the elements of his new wholeness?
    - What does Jesus not say?
32. What is Bartimaeus' faith?
    - What did he do that led Jesus to think he had faith?
    - How is this different from what is commonly

thought of as faith?

33. The next part of the verse says, literally, "and immediately he saw again." How is this different from the translation?

- What is the impact of the difference?

The last phrase—"and he followed him on the way"—may be a later editorial insertion, because this expression became a common description of those who became Christians.

STEP 2. Bridge-building

Part A

There are several ways to do bridge-building here. One way of getting the story off the page and into people is to do a role-play of the passage. The characters are Jesus, his companions (not explicitly mentioned but likely there), Bartimaeus, and the crowd. I would follow a role-play with something else, however. It could be a series of sentences to be completed. For example, "I am like Jesus in that I _____." It could be a painting of the story, putting into the scene your wounded self (parallel to the blind part of Bartimaeus), your "Jesus" self, and your "crowd" self. Or it could be a dialogue that includes you (your ego or adult) and the other parts mentioned.

Part B

Part B is the same as described in Part B of Session I (see p. 108).

STEPS 3–7

Steps 3–7 are the same as described in Session I (see pp. 108–9).

Session IV. G.P. ¶83, Luke 7:36–50 (8:1–3)

Background for Step 1

This story has a doublet in Mark 14:3–9. A doublet is a story that is similar to one in another Gospel but not parallel as we have seen in other synoptic texts. It is difficult to know whether we have two different events in these two stories, or the same event told in a very different way. Many issues are raised by this text in Luke, and the questions reflect that, but my main goal in this sequence has been to get a clear picture of the three main actors, Simon, Jesus, and the woman—what they do, think, feel, want, and sense—in this text. This makes it more likely that the use of a dialogue as a bridging exercise will be successful.

The woman in this text has been most often thought of as a (former?) prostitute, but while that is possible it is not necessarily true. Nevertheless, some of the same dynamics are at work, however she is labeled. If she is a "Sinner," with a capital S, she would serve much the same societal function she would as a Prostitute, with a capital P. We have here something similar to what we had with Bartimaeus. Just as his blindness fit into a societal-cultural framework that saw blindness as the consequence of sin, that relegated blind people to the role of beggars, that used this role as others' ticket to heaven, and that shored up the self-esteem of sighted people by labeling him Blind, with a capital B, so she too fits into a similarly complex framework. If she was a prostitute, then she did not one day just decide to do that. Nor is it likely that she emerged from the womb a prostitute. A whole set of factors are involved: the culture's definition of the place of sexual desire; the definitions of male and female roles; laws that allowed men to divorce women simply by formally saying that is what they wanted; the closing off of other gainful employment to women; women not being able to have any property; men willing to pay for sex; public condemnation but private condonation of the activity, and so on. In general, if I can say, "You're a Prostitute" (someone who uses sex to get money), then I can assure myself that I in no way would ever use sex to get what I want. And because of this societal enmeshing of the issue, it raises the question of what resistance she might face from others and what she might be able to do as a "reformed" prostitute. Where could she fit in a society set up to produce her and keep her unreformable? That is one of the issues addressed in the questions.

STEP 1. Active Listening: Luke 7:36–50 (8:1-3)

After a time of centering, have one or more participants read Luke 7:36–50.

1. Starting with the Pharisees, what do we know about them?
2. What does the invitation by the Pharisee imply about the relationship between Jesus and the Pharisee?
3. When the Pharisee issued the invitation, what might he have thought? felt? wanted?
4. What do we know about how people ate in Jesus' day?

This is a point where some information is needed if it is not forthcoming from the group. When people ate, they used a flat bread, something like a pizza crust without the sauce, as the implement with which to eat. As people ate, they would break off pieces from these large round flat "loaves," dip into the common dishes of food, and, after consuming the bread and what was on it, the part of the piece of bread they held on to would be thrown away. These pieces then became the "crumbs" that beggars had the right to pick up and eat after a meal. Because of the common pots of food, everyone who ate together had to be "clean." Clean does not mean free from dirt, but ritually clean. "Clean" people would become unclean by contact with people who were "unclean," or by contact with food touched by "unclean" people. Prostitutes were perpetually "unclean" (although men who used their services became unclean only until sundown). So if the woman who came in was thought to be a prostitute, the people assembled would likely have assumed that they had been made "unclean" when she touched Jesus, who touched the food, which touched the people.

With regard to their position at the table, people did "sit" to eat for ordinary meals. When I first read this passage in English, it was difficult to visualize how the woman could stand behind

Jesus "at his feet" if they were sitting in chairs around a table. But the Greek actually says in verses 36 and 37 that Jesus "re-clined" at table (as did the others mentioned in verse 49). People did this at more festive meals. So while Jesus' host did not do all the things a gracious host would normally do, he did some of them. Also, knowing that they were "reclining" with their feet away from the table helps us to imagine the actual setting.

5. The text, in verse 37, says, "a woman who was in the city, a sinner." What must happen in a social group for someone to be called a sinner?
   - What does this labeling do for others not labeled this way? ("You are a sinner, therefore I am. . . .")
   - What might have been her sin?
     Remember, there is more than one possible answer.
   - How could she get into being labeled this way?
   - What does this say about sin in general?
6. The text says that she knew he was reclining at the Pharisee's house. How did she know? (The text says that she was in the city, not that she was of the city.)
7. She brought an alabaster flask of ointment (perfumed liquid). What is alabaster?
   - What kind of value might it have?
8. What about the perfumed liquid?
   - What do people use perfumed liquids and ointments for in general?

See IDB, vol. III, pp. 593–95 for background.

   - What were these used for in the first century?
9. Where else are these referred to in the New Testament?

The value of such ointments is indicated by the fact that thieves took the ointment from the jars in King Tutankhamen's tomb and left behind what was later found.

10. How would she have gotten an item of such value?

In the Markan doublet, the flask of oil was valued at 300 denarii; a denarius was one day's wage of a day laborer.

11. It says she stood weeping. What might she be feeling? thinking? wanting?

In what follows, there are a series of signals that carried sexual overtones in the first century. A woman normally let her hair down only in private with her spouse, except on her wedding day, when she was carried from her father's house to the groom's house. In both cases, letting her hair down had the same implication. The word feet normally referred to the lower extremities, but the word feet was also a euphemism for genitals. The word for kissing used here meant "to fervently kiss." It was, however, not used exclusively for male-female contact. It is used also in Luke 15:20 and refers there to the father kissing his (prodigal) son on his return home. It simply indicates the intense degree of feeling. In verse 45, Jesus recognizes this when he says to Simon, "You did not kiss me, but she has not ceased to fervently kiss my feet." And finally, the ointment itself was used also for sexual purposes, as reflected in such passages as Song of Songs 5:5 and Esther 2:12.

12. In verse 38, it says that the woman did what?
13. As she did this, what might Jesus have felt? thought? wanted?
14. To allow this to happen, what would Jesus have thought about himself?
15. As she did this, what might the host and the rest of the guests have felt? thought? wanted?
16. In allowing her to continue to do these things, what does that say about Jesus in relation to the woman?
17. At this point, how would Jesus, the woman, and Simon have ranked one another in terms of importance?
18. What would have to happen for Simon's ranking to match Jesus' ranking?
19. At this point, what has happened to the meal?
20. "If this man were a prophet . . ." What does this say about Simon's thoughts about Jesus up to this moment?
    - What feelings might go with this phrase? What wants?

- Where did Simon get his expectations about Jesus as prophet?
- If Jesus turned out to be a prophet, how would Simon benefit?

21. To whom did Simon say this?
    - How did Jesus know what he was thinking?
22. What are Jesus' options at this point?
    - What different actions are open to him?
23. What has to happen in Jesus for him not to get hooked by the "*if* he were a prophet"?
24. How does this relate to the temptation experience of Jesus in the wilderness?
25. What does he actually do?
26. The first thing he does is address his host by his name (he has been anonymous up to this point). What does this do?
27. Where was the focus of people before?
    - Where is it now?

The flavor of verse 40 is lost in the translation. What it actually says is: (Jesus), "Simon, I have something to say to you"; (Simon), "Teacher—say on."

28. Putting Simon's response in your own words, what different ways could one say this?
    - How would its meaning change each time?

In the story that follows, the image, as in the Lord's Prayer, is that of indebtedness. Jewish people were not supposed to engage in the loaning-borrowing business. But it was rampant, and interest rates were even higher than they are now. This had become such a major social problem that indebtedness and sin had become virtually synonymous.

29. If indebtedness is seen as the same as sin, and the story is about the woman and Simon, what are the implications?
    - How does that differ from Simon's previous assumption?
30. In this story, loving behavior comes from what?

31. This implies that what has happened to the woman is in the past?
32. What is Simon's answer?
    - How might he have said this?
    - What might he have looked like as he said it?
    - What might Simon have been thinking? feeling? wanting?
33. How is the sequence of events at this point different from what would have happened had Jesus chosen to defend himself against the "if he were a prophet" charge?
34. During the telling of this story, what has the woman been doing?
    - What has she been thinking? feeling? wanting?
35. "Do you see this woman?" (verse 44). Did Simon see her?
    - What did Simon see?
    - What blinded Simon?
    - For Simon really to see her, what would he have to do?
    - What would have to happen in society in general?

The actions that Jesus describes, which his host failed to take, were not unusual; they were ways people commonly greeted respected guests.

36. How is Jesus interpreting the woman's actions in verses 44–46?
    - They are the outward signs of what?
37. How is this different from how Simon might have previously interpreted her actions?

Verse 47 is garbled. If we start with verse 46b, it flows easily with what has gone before—the one who has little forgiven, loves little. So far so good—a little forgiveness yields a little love. Going back to 47a, referring to the woman, the first verb says "having been forgiven"; the second verb says "she loved much." So the whole thing should probably read something like

"I tell you she showed much love because her many sins were forgiven, but little love is shown by the one to whom little is forgiven." In other words, she was forgiven *before* she came in.

38. Jesus seems to be saying that loving behavior comes from what source?

39. What might this imply about Jesus' own loving behavior? About his self-understanding?

40. In verse 48, Jesus says, "Your sins have been forgiven." The tense implies an announcement of a previous occurrence. Who might have done the forgiving? When? Where?
   ● What might have been her sins in Jesus' eyes? (He apparently does not label her behavior that we have seen in that way, as others would have.)

41. If her sins were forgiven before she came, how does that change things?
   ● Why did Jesus not mention this before?
   ● Why not do it as soon as she came in?
   ● Why wait until now?

42. If she is to be able to change, who else must change, and in what ways?

43. The others who are also reclining at table say, "Who is this, who even forgives sins? [RSV]."
   ● What are they thinking? feeling? wanting?
   ● Did Jesus say *he* forgave her?
   ● From whence does that idea come?
   ● To whom might Jesus attribute the forgiving power?
   ● In this particular situation, who needed forgiving?
   ● Who did not?

44. In verse 50, Jesus says to her, "Your faith has made you whole (healed you; saved you)." What is her faith?
   ● How did she show it?

- How is that different from what is commonly thought of as faith?
- How does this compare to Bartimaeus' faith?

45. Jesus says next, "Go in peace." How can she now go in peace more than she could before this event?

The Greek word for peace here carries the influence of the Hebrew word *shalom* with its broad connotations, including personal and societal wholeness.

- What has been added?
- What is still missing?

46. What options might be open to a reformed sinner or prostitute?

Luke 8:1–3 describes a group of people who normally would not be found together, much less travel together. It seems to be a kind of roving commune and suggests what might have happened to the woman after the event described in the previous passage. It is an option to have someone read this passage and develop some questions to draw out the implications of it. Some sample questions might be: Given the lack of precedent for this, how might they have set up the rules for this community? What might Herod's steward have thought about his wife's being in this? What does this say about how Jesus and his disciples maintained themselves? How is this different from the usual societal models?

STEP 2. Bridge-building

Part A

To build the image of how each person in this story acted, describe the sequence of things each person did. The simplest bridging exercise thereafter is to list the people (the woman, Jesus, Simon, and other guests) and have each participant complete a statement for each: "I am like/not like _____ in this passage in that I. . . ." Another fruitful exercise is to do a dialogue (as described in Chapter IV, pp. 82–83) involving each participant, the woman, Jesus, and Simon. Or one could do a dialogue with each person in the text separately. In any case, if the dialogue is used, do it in a way that involves all three principal characters. We generally need to learn from all three, especially in such a rich text as this.

Part B

Part B is the same as described in Part B of Session I (see p. 108).

STEPS 3–7

Steps 3–7 are the same as described in Session I (see pp. 108–9).

Session V

Preparation

As I mentioned before, this session in all the sequences is difficult to set up in advance. For example, it makes a difference whether you have a weekend retreat setting or a once-a-week series. In the weekend format, I assume that Session I would be Friday evening, and Sessions II, III, and IV on Saturday. This leaves Session V for Sunday morning. If this is the case, I usually do not do another Step 1 and 2. There is enough material generated from the first four sessions to work on Sunday morning.

In this sequence, it is hoped that the participants will have at least four "want" statements from previous sessions, so what is needed is time to gather these together and to reflect on them, in preparation for doing the remaining steps. If the group can gather again in a week or so, then Step 6, covenanting, can be done in the whole group; otherwise it should be done in pairs.

After the participants have done Step 6, I ask them to fill out an evaluation form. This serves to encourage further reflection on their experience, and it can be an important source of learning for the leader. The evaluation form can simply be completion of four sentences: "The part I found most helpful was. . . . The one thing I would have changed or added is. . . . The most important learning for me is. . . . Overall, the retreat (experience) for me was. . . ." After the evaluations are finished, there can be a break, and then the group reassembles about twenty minutes later for worship.

There are many options for the worship service. During a retreat, we usually do group singing between sessions; some of those songs, appropriate to the theme and group experience, can be included. I usually include communion, using a common cup and a single loaf of bread. The common cup and loaf seem to give a common focus that separate cups and pieces of bread do not. When our journey of healing is set alongside this sacrament, I find that something important happens, which I cannot adequately explain. I do not narrow the focus of the sacrament, however, to "the night when he was betrayed." Jesus broke bread with people in many different ways, including the one we looked at in Luke 7. The early church celebration recalled *all* these events and was future-oriented as well. The breaking of bread anticipated the time when all would celebrate it together in the kingdom of God, when wholeness would be restored/achieved in all creation. The other standard element in these services is a time of sharing. One way to do this is to assemble all the artwork that has been done and put it on the floor in the middle of the circle. Another is to have a time of prayer, when each person contributes as the Spirit moves her or him to do so. The one thing I do not do is give a sermon. This would seem alien to the process we have been through. However, it is appropriate for the leader to share in the same manner as other participants. And in any sharing, the ground rules still hold.

If the sequence is done in a series of weekly meetings, it may be helpful to do another Step 1 prior to moving into the other things mentioned above. The texts that follow focus on the "want" dimension as part of how we need to approach God and deepen the focus on this dimension in the previous sessions. You can use these texts also in the retreat setting, if that seems appropriate in the group's experience. My underlying assumption here is that prayer is, among other things, as I once heard Rudolf Bultmann say, "getting God to do what God would otherwise not do."

Optional Step 1

Text A: G.P. ¶147, Luke 11:5–8

A first-century home would be set up so that at night there would be a space where the household animals would be bedded down between the closed door and the father of the family. Then would come the children, the mother, and finally, the father. So for the father to move to the door involved more than just getting up and answering the door. This particular passage comes in a Lukan section on prayer and seems to be about prayer as well. After someone reads the whole text of Luke 11:5–8, it helps to get a sense of what is involved in this by having the group act this out. It's also fun to do. Everyone can get involved by having many children and a variety of animals. After, you can reassemble in the circle and get into the questions.

1. This passage is set in Luke's section on prayer. What does this have to do with prayer?
2. What does it suggest about how we need to approach God?
3. What does it suggest prayer is up against?
4. What does it imply about God?

Have someone read Psalm 44:23–26.

5. The word translated "importunity" can also be translated "impudence," "shamelessness," or "persistence." What other words would you use to describe it?
   - How is this similar to the faith of the woman in Luke 7 and Bartimaeus?
   - What does this suggest about what is needed to tap into the source of healing power?

- If we want to move toward wholeness, we have to . . . ?

Text B: G.P. ¶185, Luke 18:2–5

In this text, verse 1 seems to be an editorial introduction written by Luke or a later editor, who wanted to make sure the readers did not miss the point that this is about prayer. Prayer seems to have been one of Luke's special interests, as reflected in his insertion in the baptism narrative (Luke 3:21). Verses 6–8 seem to be dealing with the situation of the early church and to have arisen in that situation. This leaves us with verses 2–5 as the original parable. The IDB article on "Widow" gives some helpful background. A widow in that day had no legal rights and was particularly vulnerable. When her husband died, she had no share in her husband's estate. The only resource she had any claim to was the dowry she brought into the marriage. It is possible that the nonreturn of the dowry is involved here.

1. In this parable, the "praying person" is represented by whom?
   - God is represented by whom?
2. She starts out seemingly powerless, so what does she do?

The verb translated in verse 5 as "wear me out" is a vivid image. It is based on the noun that refers literally to the part of the face below the eyes. It means to strike on the parts of the body below the eyes, to beat black and blue. By extension, it refers to an energetic form of coercion. It is the word used by Paul in 1 Corinthians 9:27, where he says he believes he must take this forceful action to keep his body from getting the best of him.

3. The judge acts because he anticipates that the widow will wear him out. What does this suggest must happen for prayer to be effective?
   - What tone of voice is appropriate to this?
   - How does this contrast to the way we normally pray?
4. If God resists prayer as the judge resists the widow, what does this suggest about God?
   - What does this resistance do for the person who prays?

- If there were no resistance, what then?
5. God is seen elsewhere as like a parent. How is this judge like a parent?
   - What does that do to the image of God as a parent?
6. What does this parable say about what it takes to tap into the healing source, to move toward wholeness?

Text C: Romans 8:15
"The Spirit you have received is not a spirit of slavery leading you back into a life of fear, but a Spirit that makes us sons, enabling us to cry 'Abba! Father!' [NEB]."

There are two key words in this verse from Paul: *Kradzein,* which is translated here as "cry" and is the same word that described Bartimaeus' shouting at Jesus; and *abba,* an Aramaic word that means something like "Daddy." The word *abba,* as a way of addressing God, seems to originate with Jesus and continue into early Christianity, but the word itself is not restricted to the Aramaic language. It is but one way of formalizing the universal language of infants. It is the combination of an infant's first attempts at a consonant and vowel combination and is the same word whether it is abba or papa or dada or mama or whatever. Because of its place in the life cycle, it is clearly not a description of the qualities of the person addressed. It is rather a word that lays a claim on the person addressed. When an infant says this word, it usually means "I want _____ from you!" whether that is food or attention or changing diapers. Jesus used this address in Mark 14:36, to which we will return in the fourth sequence, but its meaning is made clear when Jesus adds, "All things are possible for you," the infant's view of "abba."

1. We have seen the Spirit in Session I on the baptism as a part of what in Jesus' life?
2. What does the Spirit do here?
3. How does this action empower us to come to God?
4. What right do we have to shout at God?
5. What does this add to the previous texts?
6. The term *abba* is the infant's address to the parent. What does it imply in this setting?
7. What does it imply for us?
8. What is added when we are told to address God both

as "abba" (the infant's address of a parent) and "Father" (the adult's address of a parent)?

STEP 2. Bridge-building

It would be possible to do a bridge-building exercise such as creating a group litany that could be used in shouted form in the worship service to follow. I have also used Walter Wink's suggestion and had the group stand with raised arms and shout the Lord's Prayer. (One time I did this, it was completely overcast outside and immediately thereafter the sky cleared with dramatic suddenness, giving way to brilliant sunshine. I would not want to guarantee this would happen again, however.) The Lord's Prayer in this format could also be incorporated into the worship experience. But it is not necessary to do a bridging exercise. The texts above can serve simply as a transition to focusing on all the previous "want" statements and as a means to enrich the completion of Steps 5–7.

CHAPTER VI

Second Sequence: "Like a Child"

Calling forth a child, he set the child in their midst and said,
"I'm telling you the truth—unless you change and become like
children, you will never enter the kingdom of heaven."
                                                    —Matthew 18:2–3

> I am a diamond necklace
> Dancing on a cloud.
> I am the biggest bumble bee,
> Going around stinging everybody.
> I am the biggest snake,
> Squeezing everybody that comes near me.
> I am an opened door going on forever.
>   —Denise Varletta, age 11[1]

Children invite mystery, they invite opportunities for the in-
congruous, the unexplained, the half-revealed, the not knowing
the impending moment, the fear of the hidden, the tension of
waiting, the anticipation of surprise, the possibility of danger,
the savoring of darkness, the games of guessing, the conditions
of secrecy. And like explorers on a perilous cliff they lean over
its edge looking for what will appear, hanging onto every surge
of suspense, frozen in their gaze, as the unexpected slowly
takes their breath away."

                                                    —Richard Lewis[2]

The "child" is born out of the womb of the unconscious, begotten out of the depths of human nature, or rather out of living
Nature herself. It is a personification of vital forces quite outside the limited range of our conscious mind, of ways and

possibilities of which our one-sided conscious mind knows nothing, a wholeness which embraces the very depths of Nature. It represents the strongest, the most ineluctable urge in every being, namely the urge to realize itself.

—C.J. Jung[3]

"What is REAL?" asked the Rabbit one day. . . .

"Real isn't how you are made," said the Skin Horse. "It's a thing that happens to you. When a child loves you for a long, long time, not just to play with, but REALLY loves you, then you become Real."

"Does it hurt?" asked the Rabbit.

"Sometimes," said the Skin Horse, for he was always truthful. "When you are Real you don't mind being hurt."

—Margery Williams, *The Velveteen Rabbit*[4]

The various stories in the Gospels which involve children clearly point to the Child in us as the key that unlocks our capacity as adults to receive the kingdom of God or to move toward wholeness. At the same time, Jesus did not elaborate much on what he meant by this. This leaves us to use our childlike imagination to ferret out what is part of that. In the first sequence, we explored the "want" dimension in us as part of what is symbolized by the Child and part of what we need to mobilize in ourselves if we are to tap into the source of healing.

The quotations at the beginning of this chapter (which you as leader can put on posters to enrich the setting for this sequence) point us to some of the other important aspects of the Child. Denise Varletta, in her poem, shows an astonishing degree of insight and nascent wholeness when she owns her "stinging" and "squeezing" parts as well as her dancing and open parts. It is as if she already knows how to be innocent as a dove *and* wise as a serpent and not to succumb to trying to be one or the other. She shows us the nascent wholeness of the Child that we adults need to recover to become more whole. The quote from C.J. Jung expands this and adds the insight that the

Child in us adults is buried in our unconscious, so that we have a real challenge in trying to recover it. Jung adds, however, that the Child is also knocking on the door of our consciousness, just waiting for us to open it.

Richard Lewis expands the symbol of the Child to include it as our bridge to the transcendent, to mystery, to the yet unknown. And this is a vitally important addition. Up to this point all the hunches, including Lewis', point to the Child as the source of healing and new growth. But that needs to be stretched. The Child in us also carries our core wounds, and because of this the Child is not just the source of healing. It is that in us which often is most in need of healing (even though that may be the source which enables us to be healers). In fact, one of the barriers that gets in our way is that just as we were once small, vulnerable, and as easily wounded as literal children, so as adults, when we get back into the Child in us and risk out of the Child in us, we somehow take on, along with the energy, spontaneity, and openness of the Child, the vulnerable and easily wounded parts. Like tender new plants emerging from the soil, new growth in us shares in that same kind of fragility and vulnerability to the forces in and around us. So it would seem that we need something more, some kind of portable protector that will shield our Child as it emerges, this time not out of the literal womb but out of the womb of the unconscious. And that is one of the issues we will be exploring in this sequence on the Child.

In his book *Ministry and Imagination*, Urban Holmes describes how he gets people in workshops to develop their imagination by writing fairy tales of their own lives. He shares one he calls "The Girl with the Red Balloon," which I have read to groups as a part of Session I of this sequence. It is a tale that carries with it much more than just the story of one woman. In a very real sense, it is a story of the human life journey. It pulls together much of what I find moving toward wholeness involves, including the risks.

Once upon a time, in a little village by the sea, lived a little girl named Lucinda. None of the people in the village called her Lucinda. They called her "that girl with the red balloon." Lucinda always carried a bright red balloon, which was tied to a long silver string, clutched tightly in her hand.

Many of the people in the village laughed at Lucinda and her red balloon. Lucinda was just a little girl, however, and it was acceptable for small children to play with red balloons.

When she was very little, Lucinda tried to explain about her red balloon. For instance, the red balloon was good for leading her somewhere—to beautiful fields, to the ocean and crashing waves, to a warm place where Lucinda felt love. But the balloon could also lead the little girl to dark mysterious caves which frightened her, or sad forests of grief which made her cry, or into the midst of quarrels. Then she felt great anger; but it all went together.

The red balloon was also excellent for seeing. If she looked at her village, her friends, or the forest through the red balloon, she saw things that others did not see. In the beginning Lucinda tried to tell others about what she saw. They laughed and Lucinda learned not to explain about her red balloon.

Lucinda was as happy as could be expected until one day someone said, "Lucinda, you are too old for a red balloon. It was okay when you were a little child, but now you are almost a woman. You must let that stupid balloon go and be mature." Lucinda held on tighter and tighter, but life became more and more difficult.

One particularly difficult day, people were saying things like: "You are always over-dramatizing with that stupid red balloon in your hand" and "If you let go of that ridiculous red balloon, you might accomplish something." Lucinda then made a decision. She knew she had to keep the red balloon, but she could hide it. The question was, where? It had to be close to her, but it had to be well hidden. So she hid the balloon inside her head.

While this hiding place fitted the criteria for closeness and secrecy, it had its disadvantages. It gave her a terrible headache. It was very difficult, as well, to laugh and shake one's head with a red balloon stuffed inside. It was also difficult to cry, to be afraid, or even to get angry. There was danger of the balloon popping out and being lost or discovered. To keep the balloon from doing this, Lucinda had to scrunch up her eyes and seeing became very difficult. So while the balloon was close, it was no longer useful for leading and for seeing.

People did stop laughing and they complimented Lucinda on her new adulthood. She got married and had babies. She even went to work in an important job in the village. Her headache got progressively worse, however, and she almost forgot about flowers, waves, warm places, caves, forests, and seeing things through red balloons.

One day, while watching her children through scrunched up eyes, she thought she saw something familiar in the hand of one of them. She tried and tried to see what it was, but she knew that if she was to really see it she would have to open wide her eyes. She knew what would happen if she did. But being a good mother and not wanting her children to have anything harmful, she did open her eyes. Just as she saw a red balloon on a silver string in the hand of her child, she cried out, and out popped her own red balloon. It looked so beautiful and it felt so good not to have that balloon in her head any more! She could see again and everything appeared as new. So Lucinda decided to leave the balloon out in the open on its silver string. She laughed and laughed and laughed.

But Lucinda did not live happily ever after. People now laugh at her and call her "spacy" and "childish," and tell her she has no common sense. The red balloon does not always lead Lucinda to beautiful fields of flowers. Dark caves are also there, as well as sad forests and quarrels. When she looks through the red balloon she does not always see beauty and happiness. But Lucinda did live *truly* ever after.[5]

The story stands beautifully on its own and needs little elaboration, although one could easily use it as a text and develop questions from it. But I do want to draw special attention to the ending, which points to the risks involved in letting the Child in us out and to the both/and quality of Lucinda's new life—laughter and tears, light and darkness—all together as a part of the conscious whole.

Before turning to the sequence itself, let us look at some

of the Old Testament background that seems pertinent to the theme of the Child. We will be returning to the creation story in Genesis 2 as a part of the next sequence, but for now I want to point out that creation stories in general tie into the Child in us in that they tell about our origins— the way things were "once upon a time," when everything was (or seemed to be) whole. In Genesis 2, Adam and Eve have many childlike qualities, such as being naked and unashamed* and being on a first-name basis with God. They are also not yet fully conscious. History, as we know it, has not yet begun. There is as yet no becoming. Much of the rest of Genesis has a similar mythic quality. It also contains many stories about our origins—the way things once were. One of the most striking is the narrative of Abraham and Sarah and the promised birth of their postmenopausal child. To hear their story, one needs to approach it imaginatively. This is no ordinary child. When Sarah hears that she is to bear a child at her age, she laughs the laughter of the adult with little faith. But she does become pregnant, and another kind of laughter is born—her child Isaac (whose name means "laughter"). Later Abraham hears from God that he is to sacrifice his child Isaac (laughter). So Abraham dutifully sets out to kill Isaac. At the last moment God's messenger says, No, killing is not the issue, but rather that you should cease to withhold your child (laughter) from God; now God can bless you.† This story can be read at many

---

*The Gospel According to Thomas reflects this in Logion 37, where it says: "His disciples said: When wilt Thou be revealed to us and when will we see thee? Jesus said: When you take off your clothing without being ashamed, and take your clothes and put them under your feet as the little children and tread on them, then [shall you behold] the Son of the Living (One) and you shall not fear." A. Guillaumont et al., The Gospel According to Thomas (New York: Harper & Bros., 1959), p. 23.
†Compare Khalil Gibran's words of The Prophet (New York: Knopf, 1958), in his segment on children, where he addresses the issue that our children are not really ours.

levels, but its movement is in many respects the same as that of "The Girl with the Red Balloon." Myths, fairy tales, and mythic history—these are ways people have shared with one another wisdom about the Child in us and what that means.

The same thing is true when we turn to stories about or visions of our final destiny. Stories of beginnings and endings have much in common. The ending stories, however, frequently have to do with the recovery of what was "in the beginning," but often without the loss of what happened "in between." The Child is not just part of our roots; it also leads us into the future. An example of this is Isaiah 11:6–9 (NEB): "[When things come together in the future,] then the wolf shall live with the sheep, and the leopard lie down with the kid; and the calf and the young lion shall grow up together, and a little child shall lead them."

As we move into the sequence itself, I'd like to add one word of caution. There is a natural tendency to idealize or sentimentalize the Child, but that is not what I understand Jesus to be getting at. He could be quite unsentimental, as in Luke 7:31–32, where he says, "How can I describe the people of this generation? What are they like? They are like [egocentric] children sitting in the market-place and shouting at each other, 'We piped for you and you would not dance.' 'We wept and wailed, and you would not mourn' [NEB]." There is a difference between becoming (as adults) "like children" and simply becoming children again. The former is the clue to our movement toward wholeness; the latter is simply regression. The goal is to be neither childish nor adultish, but to be childlike and adult-like, dovelike and serpent-like, sheeplike, and wolflike.

Session I.—G.P. ¶188, Matthew 19:13–15; Mark 10:13–16; Luke 18:15–17

Preparation for Step 1

If you have the same group for the second sequence as for the first, you may want to skip some of the things that were covered in Session I of the first sequence. But if the group includes new people, the introductory steps would be the same for this sequence as for Session I of the first sequence. Even if the group is the same, refresh people on names and repeat the ground rules. Then say a few words about the theme of this sequence and give a brief overview of the five sessions, which are:

1. The Child as the Key to Wholeness (Mark 10:13–16)
2. The Child as Risk Taker (Mark 6:1–6)
3. The Wounded Child (Mark 5:22–43)
4. The Child as the Window to the Transcendent (Mark 9:2–8)
5. The Child and the Body (John 13:1–13)

Next, brainstorm with the group to elicit the qualities and attributes they associate with the Child. For this you will need several sheets of newsprint or other large pieces of paper, and felt-tip markers. At the top of one sheet, write the word *Child*, and ask the group to come up with all the qualities they associate with this word. It is good to have two people as recorders, because the ideas usually come so fast. Put the results up around the room and then move to Step 1 of the first text. At the beginning of each Step 1, I assume that there will be at least a short time for centering and that the main text will be read out loud.

STEP 1. Mark 10:13–16 (and parallels)

A key word in this text is *hapto*, the word used for "touch." We have already met the word in Luke 7:39, where Simon uses this word to describe what the woman was doing to Jesus. Clearly, this was a significant act in Simon's mind. The word connotes more than casual contact. It was assumed that there was a definite flow of power between people when they touched in this way. In the case of the woman and Jesus, the power flow was perceived by Simon to be negative; she was unclean, and her touch made others unclean. But the power flow could go in the other direction. Someone with healing power could convey that to others by touch, as in Mark 6:56: "All those who touched [Jesus] were made whole."

1. In Mark 10:13, who are "they"?
   - What does it say they want?
   - What do they think will happen then?
   - What might they be feeling?
   - What about the children?
2. How do Matthew and Luke change this verse? Why?
3. What do we associate with the word touch?
   - What different ways of touching are there?
4. "The disciples rebuked them." The word rebuke here is the same as in the Bartimaeus story, where he is "rebuked." Why do the disciples do this?
   - What gets hooked in them?
   - What is hooking them?
   - What inner voices are they listening to?

I use this image of hooking to try to get at the action of the forces in the unconscious dimension, behind the bold vertical lines in the diagram of human interaction. It is as if they have hooks that reach out into our lives. To be effective, however, there has to be a comparable hook inside our thought world somewhere. When the two come together, our behavior is pulled around by that force. For it to be ineffective, we either have to do something about the hook of the force—defuse its power—or do something about ourselves so that there is nothing in us for the hook of the force to latch on to, or both.

5. At this point, how might the parents feel?
   - What would they be thinking? wanting?
   - And what might the children be thinking? feeling? wishing?
6. In verse 14, when Jesus saw this, he felt what?
   - What other words describe this feeling?

- The original says, literally, "And seeing, Jesus was angry." What did he see?
- Who or what might he be angry at?

7. What do Matthew and Luke do with Jesus' anger? Why?

8. How might he have said verse 14b?
   - What impact might this have had on the disciples? the parents? the children?

9. What does "to such" mean?

10. What are some of the images of the kingdom of God?
    - How might we describe this reality today? It is a place where. . . . or a time when. . . ? Or. . . ?

In verse 15, the word translated "truly" is "amen," and it means something like "this is true!" It has a much more forceful quality than "truly" seems to have today.

11. "Truly I say to you"—how would you put that in other words?
    - What is Jesus trying to convey by beginning this way?

12. There seem to be two movements in what Jesus says: receiving and entering. It is the child who needs to receive the kingdom of God. What does this say about the Child in us?
    - If we are to "receive" it, what does this say about the kingdom?
    - It is "doing" what?
    - The "whoever" links back up to the verb enter. What part of us is addressed by the "whoever"?
    - So the kingdom is also . . . ?

13. Verse 16 says what?
    - On what other occasions did Jesus lay hands on people?
    - Why does he do that here?

STEP 2. Bridge-building

For the bridge-building exercise, the participants might draw their own inner Child with crayons (or, if they are not sighted, some other media associated with children, such as finger paints). They should be encouraged to be as unconstrained as possible—their child can have three eyes or two noses or whatever. When they have done this, ask them to gather in groups of three or four and go through three steps: (1) introduce their child to the other "children"; (2) talk about who the disciple in them is and how this part of them rebukes the child; (3) share who the Jesus in them is that wants to draw the child into the center of things as a source of healing and to be healed.

As a wrap-up to this session, I suggest reassembling the whole group and reading the story of Lucinda. If the group meets weekly, you may want to do Steps 3–6 and then use the Lucinda story, if it seems appropriate.

STEPS 3–7

Steps 3–7 are the same as described on pages 108–9.

Session II. G.P. ¶108, Mark 6:1–6; Matthew 13:53–58

Preparation and Background for Step 1

For this passage it is important for both leader and group to sketch in the main things that have happened to Jesus prior to this event. The first step is Jesus' leaving home. His father had probably died when he was in his teens. This would have left him, as the oldest male child in the family, with some of the responsibilities of the father. If he was around thirty when he left home (as it seems reasonable to assume), his youngest sibling by that time would probably have reached the age of adult responsibility (twelve to fourteen years old). Nevertheless, leaving home, coupled with what he left home *for*, would have represented a significant breaking of normal life patterns of the time. Then comes Jesus' baptism, with all that this event meant to him, including getting a new set of parents. Next is his trial by fire in the wilderness, where he did an initial sorting through of what it might mean to be a child of God and of the Spirit. After this comes his gathering of the disciples and his initial successes on the road as teacher and healer. Sprinkled in here were two apparent attempts by hometown people to get him to cease what he was doing. In Mark 3:21, his friends (or relatives, depending on how the Greek is interpreted) set out to seize, or take charge of, Jesus, because the word was out that Jesus was "beside himself." The Greek word used here is the one from which we get the word ecstasy. It means, literally, "to stand out of one's self." Even today Webster's first definition is "a state of being beyond reason and self-control."[6] In the context in Mark 3:21, it probably means they thought he was crazy or had lost his mind. But the same word can be used to express a state of intense emotion or awe, as in Mark 4:41, where the disciples were awed by the calming of the water. It seems to depend on which part of the "elephant" you are focusing on. In Mark 3:31–35, his mother and brothers and sisters sought him, but again he rejected their seeking. In spite of this, he later chooses to risk going home. Jesus must have been aware of the situation he would face from the previous visits of hometown people, but there is also the common risk we all take when we go home—we always go as children.

STEP 1. Mark 6:1–6; Matthew 13:53–58

1. Verse 1 says that Jesus came to his *patrida*, his home country, or hometown, or territory of his family. What is it like to go home after the kinds of new and powerful experiences that Jesus has been through?
2. Why would Jesus want to go home?
3. What would he be thinking? feeling?
4. Why did he take his disciples with him?

Time passes between verses 1 and 2. Jesus would have arrived home prior to the sabbath. He probably would not have traveled on the sabbath, and he also would have had to check in with the synagogue chief to get his permission to speak in the synagogue on the sabbath.

5. We are not told what Jesus said. What might he have shared with these people?

6. The people's response is one of astonishment. The Greek word means, literally, "they were struck out of their senses." The closest we have to this today is "he blew their minds." There is a strong element of fear in the word. Why might they be afraid (threatened)?
    - If they took him seriously, how would they have to change?

7. The people's response in verse 2 gives us a clue to their reaction and to what Jesus was saying before. Try to put these words of the people into words we would use today. How might they have said them?
    - What were they thinking? feeling? wanting?

8. Such powerful deeds through *his hands*—what were they accustomed to seeing *his hands* do?
    - What does this tell us about what is happening?

9. They seem to be saying, "Who does he think he is?" Who *does* he think he is?
    - Who do they think he is? (Verse 4)

10. What are the feelings behind the words in verse 4? the thoughts? the wants?
    - What is hooking them?

11. The last part of verse 4 says, literally, "and they were scandalized by him." In other words, they radically *reject* him. Now presumably he has just shared with them something of his recent profoundly meaningful experience, and he gets put down hard. At this point, what might Jesus be feeling? thinking? wanting?

12. Setting aside what you know about what Jesus actually did next, what were his options at this point?
    - What could he have done?
    - What would you have done after being so thoroughly rejected?

13. Jesus replies, "A prophet is not dishonored except in his *patrida* (home area), among his relatives, and in his own home." The first question is, again, Who does he think he is?
14. Before, when he spoke in the temptation narrative, his wisdom came from where?
15. Now we get a different source. Jesus' reply is a quotation, but it is not from scripture. It comes from the popular, broadly accepted collection of folk wisdom. A parallel today would be something like "Haste makes waste." Where do we learn these kinds of sayings?
16. To whom is this saying addressed?
    ● Whom else?
17. Which part of Jesus is speaking?
18. What can we learn from this about the option Jesus chooses?
19. Whose problem is the people's reaction in the first place?
20. How does Jesus' action address that?
21. Where did he get the internal security to react this way and not in other ways?
    ● How does he avoid getting hooked himself?
22. Verse 5 says what?
    ● Why could he do no powerful deeds?
    ● What was missing?
    ● Whose problem was it?

Matthew reworks the ending to give his hunch.

23. In verse 6, "marveled" (RSV) is a bit strong: it is more like mild surprise. As he said this, what might he have been thinking? wanting?

STEP 2. Bridge-building

Jesus seems to have moved through this experience of risking out of his inner Child without succumbing to the various temptations that lie close at hand when our Child gets put down. The key to the bridge-building seems to lie in ferreting out steps in the process. What did he do to be able to pull this off so well? The steps seem to have been the following: He had some forewarning that there might be risk involved, that his hometown people might react negatively to his return. He knew he was going home as a child, but he wanted to go home anyway. He took along his own support group, he took along his grounding in his new "Parents"—God and the Spirit—and he took along his own internal wisdom figure, who could advise when his Child got in a bind.

From this, a number of bridge-building exercises can emerge. One effective exercise is to create a "trialogue" (in silence and on paper) between one's self, one's parents(s) or hometown folk, and one's own internal wisdom source. To get a fix on a wisdom figure, focus on a particular person who represents that wisdom figure or who has played that role in the past. It might be a grandparent or uncle or friend or some figure from history, such as Jesus or Gandhi. I suggest starting the trialogue by saying "Dad/ Mom/etc., I've never told you this, but what I really want to say (ask/share) is. . . ." Then allow the conversation to continue with the wisdom figure coming in when needed.

When people are ready, invite them to share.

STEPS 3-7

Steps 3–7 are the same as described on pages 108–9.

Session III. G.P. ¶107, Matthew 9:18–26; Mark 5:21–43; Luke 8:40–56

Preparation and Background for Step 1

Because this is a long text, involving a story within a story, I do not ask many questions related to the variations in Matthew and Luke from Mark's narrative and I do not ask as many questions on the text itself.

Each story could be said to deal with a wounded child. The one deals with a father interceding on behalf of his daughter, the other with a woman interceding on behalf of her wounded Child within, as it were. We've already talked about the word touch and seen other children on whom Jesus laid his hands. The power flow that touch set in motion is even more an issue here. Both the woman (because of her flow of blood) and the child (if she were really dead) would have been unclean, and the assumption would be that Jesus would have been made unclean in both cases. Jesus, in risking touching the girl, and the woman in daring to touch Jesus, would have had to assume that the opposite would in fact occur—that a healing power would flow out of Jesus and he would not become unclean. In any case, the word touch (like laying on of hands) points to a substantial touch, not a light or casual touch.

The other critical piece of background has to do with the consequences of the woman's condition. This condition would have put her in a situation of severe isolation from normal life for the whole twelve-year period. She could not touch or be touched by anyone, and she could not even touch things that others would touch (see Leviticus 15:19–30). Objects that she touched, which others would thereafter use, would have had to be purified first. Some objects, like clay pots, would have had to be destroyed. As she moved through the crowd, she presumably made many people unclean along the way. On top of the isolation caused by her uncleanness came the rigors, the expense, and the demeaning nature of the cures that would have been tried on her. Some of the many cures she might have been subjected to are: "Take three measures of Persian onions, boil them in wine, have the women drink it and say to her, 'Get up and leave your flow of blood behind!'" Or "Have her sit down on a fork in the road and have her take a glass of wine in her hand; then someone should come up behind her (without her knowledge), scare her and say 'Get up and leave your flow of blood behind!'" Or "Dig seven holes in the ground and burn, in each one, grape vines that are no more than three years old; after this, she should take a glass of wine in her hand. Then have her sit in one hole and get up, sit in another and get up, and so on through each of the seven holes in the ground. Each time, in the very moment she gets up, you should say, 'Get up and leave your flow of blood behind!'" Or "You take fine flour, apply it to the lower half of her body and say to her 'Get up and leave your flow of blood behind!'" All the cures described have one thing in common—the healing agent did not touch her. And in most of them, including many not mentioned, very expensive elements, such as imported herbs, were used.[7]

STEP 1. Mark 5:21–43 (and parallels)

1. Starting with verse 22, it says what?

> The action of falling at the feet of Jesus is a rare occurrence in the Gospels. The only other place it occurs in Mark is in Mark 7:25, where the gentile woman does it while begging Jesus to heal her daughter. (The woman in this story does something like it without mention of feet.) The status of Jairus as synagogue chief makes the action all the more striking.

2. Imagine yourself falling at someone's feet. What would it feel like?
    - If someone did that to you, what would the impact on you be?
    - What does this action tell about Jairus?
3. Jairus implores Jesus to do what?
    - He is very specific and clear about what he wants and what he expects will happen. Why might this be important?

- How does this compare to our approach to people in the healing professions?
4. What does Jesus risk by going with Jairus?

We need to put this story on hold now, while we deal with the story in the middle.

5. In verse 25, we are told about a woman who has had a flow of blood for twelve years. What would have been the consequences of this for the woman, apart from what we are told in the next verse?

Some background may be needed from the leader here.

6. In addition to the social consequences of her condition, we are told what in verse 26?
7. What could have sustained her through all those years?
    - At this point, what is your image of this woman?
8. She had heard about Jesus. What would she have heard?
9. In moving through the crowd, what risk was she taking?
10. In touching Jesus' garment, what could have happened?
    - What did she assume would happen?
11. In verse 28, we are told about what she said to herself. What part of her was speaking to what other part of her?
12. This mental image seems to correspond to Jairus' mental image reflected in verse 23. What is the importance of having this?
    - What does it do for the person seeking healing? For the release of healing power from the other person?

Contrast Jesus' hometown people.

13. In verse 29, her *body* is "cured"; what is not yet healed?

"Cured" is a more limited word than the one we've seen before, which I have translated "healed" or "saved" or "made whole."

14. Jesus sensed the power flow. How?
15. Why did he seek her out?
    - What is at stake?
16. How do the disciples respond?
    - What voice do the disciples represent?
17. How does Jesus respond to their comment?
18. The woman comes in "fear and trembling." Why?
    - What is she afraid of? What else?
19. She tells Jesus *all* the truth. Who is listening?

Luke fills in a general hunch.

    - Why is it important for her to do this?
20. What does this add to her healing?
    - What does this say about the healing process in general?
    - Moving toward wholeness involves what?
21. Jesus says, "Your faith has made you whole [healed you/saved you]." What is her faith?
22. In the second part of this verse, Jesus says, "Go in peace [*shalom*], and be safe from [all] that has plagued [troubled] you." What is she now safe from?

Now we take the first story out of hold.

23. Shifting our focus, at what point did we leave the story of Jairus?
24. In verse 35, the messengers come with what message?
25. What are Jairus' choices at this point?
26. If she were dead and Jesus went ahead and touched the girl, what would people assume?
27. Jesus overhears them and says to Jairus, "Do not fear; have faith!" "Faith" for Jesus here is what?
28. In verse 37, he takes Peter, James, and John with him. Who does he leave behind? Why?
    - What does this add to our understanding of what facilitates/hinders healing?

The weeping and wailing were required activities when someone died. You were obligated to have at least one flute player
and one wailing woman (both professionals) to stimulate the
outward signs of grieving.

29. Focus for a minute on the two words dead and sleep-
    ing. What image do we get with the word dead?
    - With the word sleeping?
    - The word for sleeping means a deep sleep or, in
      today's vocabulary, probably a coma. When
      someone slips into a coma, what do we assume?
    - What does Jesus assume?

30. The people ridicule Jesus. What in them is speaking?

31. Jesus puts them all out except the father, mother, and
    three disciples. Why?

32. The girl is unconscious, but Jesus does what?
    - How does she hear him?
    - He treats her as if she were what?
    - How does that contrast with the reaction of
      others?
    - What is the importance of this stance?

33. In verse 42, it says she got up and walked (because)
    she was twelve years old. What might we have ex-
    pected after the "because"?

34. The people were, literally translated, "beside them-
    selves" (the same word was applied to Jesus before,
    meaning "gone crazy," "lost his mind") with im-
    mediate "beside-themselvesness," if one could say
    that. They were absolutely amazed. Was Jesus?

35. Why would it be important for the girl that Jesus not
    be amazed?

36. Where is she coming from?

37. The last thing he says is, "Give her something to eat."
    It seems like such a low-key ending. What is the
    significance of this?
    - How is this consistent with Jesus' actions
      throughout?

- How does this expand our understanding of healing?

STEP 2. Bridge-building

In this text I break my rule that Step 2 should enable people to identify with all the people or parts of a text. For one thing, there are a lot of people and two stories. But what is more important, I want especially to draw out the wounded child part of each person, so I simply ask each participant to draw or paint his or her wounded child. This exercise generally puts people in touch with some painful parts of their lives, but this is usually a liberating and healing experience. When it comes time for sharing, there may be some tears and strong feelings. My strategy in this kind of setting is to give people space, to treat this expression of feeling as normal, just as Jesus treated the little girl as normal and in a matter-of-fact manner.

When people are ready, invite them to share.

STEPS 3–7

Steps 3–7 are the same as described on pages 108–9.

Session IV. G.P. ¶124, Matthew 17:1–8; Mark 9:2–8; Luke 9:28–36

Preparation and Background for Step 1

This text has presented a problem to those who would interpret its meaning, because it shows the transcendent dimension breaking into daily life. Many scholars have been inclined to solve the problem by seeing this text as a postresurrection story or as generated in the postresurrection time. I prefer to leave it where Mark put it and take it from there. My own approach includes two working assumptions: (1) that the transcendent does break into ordinary life in ways not unlike what happens in this text, an assumption based in part simply on personal experience, and (2) that this story is best understood by placing it in Jesus' (preresurrection) story of becoming; that is, it either actually took place in that setting (my personal hunch) and/or it was intentionally placed *there* (right where it is) by Mark. It is a judgment call one way or the other. Having said that, the rest of this section will be devoted to background information designed to help understand the text in the setting in Mark in which we find it.

The first thing to do is to read through the text until you get to the punch line, which seems to be "This is my Son, my loved one. Listen to him." The same words were in Mark's version of the baptism, with two exceptions: "You" is now "this" and the words "listen to him" are new. So if this is the solution; what is the problem? Perhaps people were *not* listening to Jesus and he was frustrated. In fact, even Jesus' disciples seem to have not been listening. If we go through Mark, we find many instances where people did not listen and many indications of Jesus' frustration at this. We have already looked at the reaction of Jesus' hometown people. Let us note references to the issue of listening:

[Jesus]: Listen! . . . If you have ears to hear, then hear [Mark 4:3, 9, NEB].

[Jesus]: You [the disciples] do not understand this parable? How then are you to understand any parable? [Mark 4:13, NEB].

[Jesus]: He said to them [disciples] . . . "If you have ears to hear, then hear." He also said, "Take note of what you hear" [Mark 4:21, 23, 24, NEB].

[The disciples] had not understood the incident of the loaves; their minds were closed [Greek: hearts hardened] [Mark 6:52, NEB].

[Jesus] said to them, "Are you as dull as the rest?" [Mark 7:18, NEB].

Prior to the next quotation, Jesus had spoken metaphorically about the "leaven of the Pharisees." The disciples had forgotten to bring bread along, so Jesus' words were not heard, at least not as Jesus intended.

So the disciples had a rational (left-brained) discussion among themselves about the loaves they had forgotten. And knowing them, Jesus said to them, "Why are you carrying on a rational discussion about not having the bread? Don't you get it yet? Don't you understand yet? Have your hearts been hardened (i.e., Have you shut down the right hemisphere of your brains)? Having eyes, can't you see? Having ears, can't you hear? (Mark 8:16–18).

Even if some of these quotations reflect Mark's editorial work, they would still point to why Mark put the story of the transfiguration where it is. But it seems to me that the issue of not being heard does reflect Jesus' experience. He was often misunderstood, and I am sure it was frustrating to him. The final quotation is especially illuminating. The hardening of the heart is a classic biblical expression that indicates a shutdown of the imagination, of feelings, and of the capacity to be touched by the transcendent claim of God. The disciples were using only a limited part of their awareness. The heart, in general, seems to open or close eyes and ears, depending on its condition, and for this passage about the transfiguration it is advisable to have one's heart in healthy, pliable condition.

The issue of listening is a clue to the appearance of Elijah and Moses. They are generally not expected to appear together, especially out of order. So why are they the ones who appear? What internal need of Jesus calls forth this particular pair? What did they have to talk about? (We read that they talked, but not what about, except for Luke, who has one idea about that.) Both Elijah and Moses were seen as prophets (the one self-designation Jesus seems to have accepted, in addition to Rabbi); both were called on to speak God's message in their time; and both had problems with their audiences. Starting with Moses, it is instructive to read through the parts about speaking and listening (for example, Exodus 3:18; 4:1; 4:10–17; 6:9; 6:28–30; 7:3–4; 7:13; 7:22; 8:15; 8:19; 11:9; 12:33 (Pharaoh finally listens). In reading through this, it becomes almost a kind of litany (God to Moses: "Speak!" Moses to God: "I can't speak and/or they will not listen." Moses speaks; they don't listen). Apart from the frustration that the speaker must experience, the question arises, What is the role of resistance? What happens if people hear right away and respond right away? One way or the other, Moses had extensive experience related to the issue of listening and may have gleaned some wisdom about that and the function of resistance to what he had to say.

Elijah had resistance problems also. Jezebel was an especially irascible listener to what Elijah had to say. She did more than just resist Elijah's wisdom. What Elijah adds to what Moses experienced is that when things got especially difficult for him, Elijah retreated to a mountaintop and had some numinous experiences there (1 Kings 19). So the experience of these two wisdom figures, with which Jesus would certainly have been familiar, would have made them good people to turn to on a mountaintop retreat to reflect on the issues of speaking and listening.

When I first started working on the transfiguration text, the part that seemed odd was Peter's response in verse 5. It seemed to be one of those "What-do-you-say-when-you-don't-know-what-to-say?" responses, as Mark tries to explain. But think about the mountaintop setting (reminiscent of Sinai), the shining appearance of Jesus (like that of Moses on Mount Sinai; Exodus 34:29, 34–35), and the appearance of Moses himself, along with the annual experience of the Feast of the Tabernacles, which commemorated these very memories. Taken together, they do seem to make this response of Peter's more understandable. (The Greek word translated "booth" verse 5 can also be translated "tent" or "tabernacle.") Exodus 33:7–11 makes this even more clear and provides a link to the last piece of background. It reads:

Moses used to take a tent and pitch it at a distance outside the camp. He called it the Tent of the Presence, and everyone who sought the Lord would go out to the Tent of the Presence outside the camp. . . . When Moses entered it, the *pillar of cloud* came down, and stayed at the entrance to the tent while the Lord spoke with Moses. . . . The Lord would speak to Moses face to face. . . [NEB].

In this passage is one of many references to the appearance of a cloud, coupled with the experienced presence of God. The Israelites were guided on their wilderness journey by a cloud (Exodus 13:21–22). A cloud protected the Israelites from the Egyptians (Exodus 14:19–20). It appeared when God spoke to Moses in response to the people's complaints (Exodus 16:10). It appeared when God spoke "in the hearing of the people, [so that] their faith in you [Moses] may never fail [Exodus, 19:9, NEB]." It also appeared on Mount Sinai itself, when Moses spoke with God (Exodus 20:19–21; 24:15–18). The most striking of these passages is in Exodus 19:9, where the cloud accompanies an appearance by God to reassure Moses and reinforce Moses' credibility and authority.[8]

In leading this text, use some of the above background material. Most people do not have this kind of information readily available. Background can be given either before getting into the questions (and after the text from Mark has been read out loud), or it can be woven in at points where it comes up. It can still be done in the style we've been using by having the participants look up and read the various sections.

STEP 1. Mark 9:2–8 (and parallels)
1. Where have we seen these three disciples before?
   - Why does Jesus take only these three along, and not the other nine?

- Why does he not go alone?

2. Why do people go to "high mountains apart by them-selves"?

3. Why might Jesus be doing this at this time?
   - What do wildernesses and mountains have in common?
   - What issues might have been on his mind at this time?
   - What historical memories would a mountain setting trigger?

4. "He was transfigured before them"—before whom is this taking place?
   - What are they seeing?
   - What might they be thinking? feeling? wanting?
   - What historical memories might be coming into play here?

5. Verse 3 says what?
   - Focusing on his whole appearance (face, clothing, etc.?), what does this say about what is going on inside Jesus?
   - In other words, he looks as if he is . . . ?

6. In verse 4, Elijah and Moses appear. What do we know about these two figures?
   - What inner need of Jesus' might have summoned these two (as opposed to other wisdom figures)?
   - About what might they have been talking to Jesus? (What is Luke's guess?)
   - How did the disciples know who they were?

7. What do you make of Peter's response in verse 5?
   - What else could he have said?
   - If Jesus had been talking about (what), then Peter was (what)?

8. Mark explains Peter's response. Why?
   - Mark also says that they became very afraid. Of what?

- Compare Matthew and Luke. How do you account for the changes (omissions)?
9. In verse 9, a cloud casts a shadow over them and a voice comes out of the cloud. What do we know from the Old Testament about clouds like this?
   - What is a cloud like?
   - What part of God might this be?
10. The voice says what?
    - What does this say about why Jesus might have gone up the mountain?
    - To whom is this message addressed?
    - For whom is this message?
11. If the disciples were not listening before, why were they not listening?
    - What positive role might their resistance have played?
    - How might Moses and Elijah have helped Jesus?

STEP 2. Bridge-building

For the bridging exercise, ask the participants to take pencil and paper and go through several steps: (1) Think of some place, like the mountain in this story, where you have had a strong sense of God's presence. (2) Imagine taking an issue in your life you are wrestling with right now to this place. (3) Bring into this setting the wisdom figure that can best help you with that issue; it could be a friend or relative, or even a historical figure. (4) Begin a dialogue with your wisdom figure about your issue. Once the dialogue is finished, write down what you can remember.

When people are ready, invite them to share.

STEPS 3–7

Steps 3–7 are the same as described on pages 108–9.

Session V. John 13:1–13

Preparation

Because this whole sequence can surface many deep-seated feelings and some strong wants and can lead to some important learnings, the main task of this final session is to pull together what has gone before in the first half of the session so that people can complete Steps 3 through 7. One way to do this is to talk through the previous four sessions, asking questions about each one (In the first session we did what? What else? In the second session we did what? etc.). One interim step here also would be to use the Lucinda story. On a piece of newsprint, you could record what the group sees as the main steps in the process Lucinda went through. It is hoped that the first four sessions served the function of the Child in the story that sprang loose Lucinda's balloon. The question then becomes, What is being sprung loose in each of us right now, and what do we want to do with it now that it is out? After having people fill out the evaluation forms, you are ready for the second part of the session.

In the worship phase John 13 can be used, not as a Step 1 in the sense that we have been doing it, but as a worship guide. Whatever the actual historical setting of John 13, one thing is clear: The Jesus of this text washed the disciples' feet (just as his had been washed by the woman) and he says (verse 15), "I want you to do what I have done." If there was ever a time to get people to tap into their inner Child and actually risk doing this, this is it. The mechanics of this have to be well thought out. People have to be forewarned so that they can wear appropriate clothing and bring towels and washcloths. We used buckets with warm water with a small amount of mild detergent in the water. We dipped washcloths in the water and cleansed one another's feet. After towel-drying the feet, we applied a perfumed skin lotion. To do this in a worshipful way, we have to deal with the inner Peter that says, "No way am I going to get into this!" It also needs to be voluntary, so that no one is put under pressure.

The other elements of the worship are similar to what I described in the last chapter. I would definitely include communion; that was the kind of setting in John 13. And I would include a time for verbal sharing as well as some singing.

And remember, "A little child shall lead [Isaiah 11:6, NEB]."

CHAPTER VII

Third Sequence:
Deepening Our Spiritual Journey

There are many more worlds than one, and in many ways they are unlike each other. But . . . good and evil are not absent in their degree from any of the worlds, for wherever there is life there is action, and action is but the expression of one or other of these qualities.

—James Stephens[1]

Eyes must be opened to inner reality. Such an "opening of one's eyes," a "revelation," can never be given directly in so many words. We see inner reality only through an "aha!" experience, a sudden insight into our own being. There is no way to describe inner reality directly.

—John Sanford[2]

The most profound human questions are the ones that give rise to creation myths: Who are we? Why are we here? What is the purpose of our lives and our deaths? How should we understand our place in the world, in time and space? . . . [Old myths] have been challenged not by new facts but by new attitudes toward facts; they have been challenged by new myths.

—Barbara Sproul[3]

The unconscious is not only the basement of our minds into which we place the discarded material of our lives; it is also the ocean out of which our conscious lives have sprung, and over which the ships of our souls sail their course through life.

—John Sanford[4]

No man or woman, no matter how profound he or she may be, can say beyond a doubt that this or that IS the Kingdom of God.
                                                                    —Robert Schwenck[5]

"Does it [becoming Real] happen all at once . . . [asked the Rabbit] or bit by bit?"
"It doesn't happen all at once," said the Skin Horse. "You become. It takes a long time. That's why it doesn't happen to people who break easily, or have sharp edges, or who have to be carefully kept. Generally, by the time you are Real, most of your hair has been loved off, and your eyes drop out and you get loose in the joints and very shabby. But these things don't matter at all, because once you are Real you can't be ugly, except to people who don't understand."
                                         —Margery Williams, *The Velveteen Rabbit*[6]

In the first two sequences, the focus was on the Child as the part of us that "receives" the kingdom of God, as the part of us that leads us into the kingdom, and as the wounded healer in us that both is in need of healing and moves us toward healing. In this sequence, the focus shifts more to the "whoever" that is to enter the kingdom of God, as well as the kingdom of God itself. As the last quotation above, from *The Velveteen Rabbit*, suggests, this sequence attempts to address the bit-by-bit part of becoming Real.

In the history of scholarly work with the New Testament, few subjects have generated more debate than the kingdom of God. Whole groups of scholars have clustered around one point of view or another—whether the kingdom is only in the future, now and in the future, starting now and continuing into the future, and so on. But in general this way of focusing on the issue has not been particularly fruitful.[7]

In attempting to formulate the issue differently, the Markan summary of Jesus' message gives us an important clue: "The time is fulfilled, the kingdom of God is at hand; [so] repent [Mark 1:15, RSV]." What does Jesus hope for (want) in terms of a human response here? If I had a baseball in my hand and I announced as I was about to toss it to you, "This baseball is at hand," you would presumably adapt yourself (repent) and get in the appropriate position to catch it. That is the same kind of process at work in Jesus' message. His concern was with the process (repentance) that it takes to get ready for, to receive, and so on, the kingdom. As Norman Perrin says, "[The kingdom] is to be found wherever God is active decisively within the experience of an individual."[8] It is, however, not just a one-time thing; it is a process that repeats itself. It is as if Jesus were to say to us, "Peace is at hand." If we believed him and started acting more peacefully, then peace would indeed be more at hand than it was previously. But it is very easy to move again into less peaceful behaviors, and so we need to hear the message ever anew and respond again and again.

The kingdom itself is like truth, a reality that is "out there," and like truth it is something that cannot be defined once and for all. When Jesus spoke of it, he either assumed that people knew what it was, as in Mark 1:15, where he speaks of the nearness of the kingdom, or when he tried to convey something about the nature of the kingdom he used the language of simile, metaphor, and symbol. He never said, "The kingdom of God is . . ." followed by a definition of the kingdom. He always said, "The kingdom of God is like. . . ." And this way of speaking about it is so understandable because it is the kind of language humans have always resorted to when speaking about the ultimate realities of life.[9] The kingdom is so difficult to define (what it "really" is) because it represents or symbolizes that toward which all life or history itself is moving at its best. It is the response to the (ultimately unanswerable) question "What would life look like if it looked the way it ought to look?" In attempting to respond to this question, people throughout history have turned to stories about how things were "in the beginning" or "once upon a time" and to stories about how things will be "in the end."

In putting together this sequence, therefore, I began with stories about beginnings. The obvious place to start would have been with one of the creation stories in Genesis, but I chose to start with creation stories from other cultures as a means of helping people appreciate the kind of material found in Genesis. The scientific mind-set is so contaminating that it takes a special effort to be released from its thrall and be able to hear a story like that in Genesis 2 the way it was intended to be heard. I chose the creation narrative in Genesis 2 instead of the account of creation in Genesis 1 because Genesis 2 is more of a story while Genesis 1 is more of a poem or hymn. Genesis 1 is more of a pure theological statement, whereas Genesis 2 deals with people who interact, who relate to one another and to God, and who symbolize the beginnings of the life journey of us as human beings.

The next part of the sequence focuses specifically on the process of change in ourselves that occurs as we respond to the reality with which such stories put us in touch. In Session IV, we look at some of Jesus' stories (parables) about the kingdom. The wrap-up session is set up to help people individualize and respond to a piece of the kingdom for themselves.

You will discover that the method I have been using is expanded to include material from other cultures as well as some other things that can enrich the experience. The method itself is also somewhat more flexible.

In preparing to lead this sequence, I suggest further reading in three of the books quoted at the beginning of this chapter: Barbara Sproul's *Primal Myths* contains an excellent introduction to and an illuminating sampling of creation stories from around the world; John Sanford's *The Kingdom Within* is one of the most stimulating works on this subject; and Robert Schwenck's *Digging Deep* helps deepen appreciation of key images used in the creation stories.

Session I. "In the Beginning . . ."

Preliminaries to Step 1

The first two sequences are intended to precede this one. In that case the introduction to the method and some of the other introductory material can be omitted. However, post the ground rules and go over them sometime during the first part of this session.

After the participants gather in a circle, ask them to recall in silence a fairy tale or nursery rhyme and to stay with the very first one that comes to mind. After they have had time to do this, ask them to fill out in their minds what they remember of it. People will recall the same fairy tale or nursery rhyme in different ways. What I am looking for in this is the tale or rhyme *as they remember it* (to avoid debate about the way it is supposed to go and because there is a significance for the individual in the way it is remembered). After everyone has shared, ask people to think about how their life stories are or have been like the story or rhyme they have shared. Next ask the group members to jot down some notes for themselves about the links they have discovered between the stories or rhymes and their lives. If people seem to be struggling with this, you could take a couple of volunteers through their stories to illustrate the process. Finally, have the participants share what they have discovered in groups of two or three.

> The purpose of this first part is to help the group members see how they can link up stories, similar to ones we will be looking at later, with their lives and learn something meaningful about themselves from this linkage. I chose fairy tales or nursery rhymes because just about everyone has a memory of one and the ones people remember seem to say something significant about their own life stories.

After this exercise, present an overview of the five sessions as you have set them up, along with some of the material included in the introduction to this chapter as it seems appropriate. You may also put in a reminder about the ground rules here.

To foster the kind of "is like" thinking that is needed to get into creation stories, I have selected some of the key objects and words that will appear in the various stories at which we will be looking. I suggest putting these up one at a time on newsprint and asking the participants to think of the various things, images, and metaphors they associate with them. These are: rocks/stones; trees; seeds; wind; water; fire; moon; sun; fish; naked; height/high; depth/deep; fruit; rise; fall; snakes; earth/ground; pearls.

Ask the group members to spend some time outside between Session I and Session II to find some object in nature that speaks to them, to think how they are like that object, and to bring it (if it is portable) to Session II. You can then begin Session II with people sharing what they have found.

STEP 1. The Salmon People, the Bear People, and the River

Like other stories about beginnings, the story that follows from the Native Americans of the Northwest is a story about you and me. It is also, in a sense, a story about the kingdom of God and what it takes to enter it.

The leader reads the story aloud.

Before there were any people walking around this valley there were bear people. They had an agreement with the salmon. . . . The salmon would come upriver every fall and the bears would acknowledge this and take what they needed. This is the way it was with everything. Everyone lived by certain agreements and courtesies. But the salmon people and the bear people had made no agreement with the river. It had been overlooked. No one thought it was even necessary. . . . One fall the river pulled itself back into the shore trees and wouldn't let the salmon enter from the ocean. Whenever they would try, the river would pull back and leave the salmon stranded on the beach. There was a long argument, a lot of talk. Finally, the river let the salmon enter. But when the salmon got up into this country where the bears lived, the river began to run in two directions at once, north on one side, south on the other, roaring, heaving white water, and rolling big boulders up on the banks. Then the river was suddenly still. The salmon were afraid to move. The bears were standing behind trees, looking out. The river said in the middle of all this silence that there had to be an agreement. No one could just do something, whatever they wanted. You couldn't just take someone for granted.

So for several days, they spoke about it. The salmon said who they were, and where they came from, and the bears spoke about what they did, what powers had been given, and the river spoke about its agreement with the rain and the wind and the crayfish and so on. Everybody said what they needed and what they would give away. Then a very odd thing happened—the river said it loved the salmon. No one had ever said anything like this before. No one had taken this chance. It was an honesty that pleased everyone. It made for a very deep agreement among them.

Well, they were able to reach an understanding about their obligations to each other and everyone went his way. This remains unchanged. . . . [So] when you feel the river shuddering against your legs, you are feeling the presence of all these agreements.[10]

1. There were no people, but there were bear people and salmon people. What does this tell us about the why of this story?
2. Where do the bear and salmon people live?
3. What might these two places represent?
4. From what does the bear live?
    - What does the salmon need to live?
    - What had been overlooked?
    - What might this represent in ourselves?
5. What bodies of water were significant in the Bible?

- What did they represent?
6. What do you make of the river's protest?
    - Why did it protest?
    - What did it feel? want?
    - What in us might give off signals that are similar?
    - What triggers this signal system?
7. What effect did this protest have on the bear and the salmon?
    - How did they feel?
    - What did they think?
8. What was wrong, according to the river?
    - What is an agreement?
    - What is the biblical word for agreement?
    - Why are these important?
    - What do they make possible that would not be possible otherwise?
9. What first steps were taken to move out of the destructive situation and toward a better one?
    - How would you describe these steps in other ways?
10. The breakdown came at what point?
11. Going back, how did the river show its love before?
    - What did that action feel like to the salmon and the bear?
12. What was the outcome of the river's action?
    - What is there now that was not there before?
    - What did it take to get to that point?
13. What message does the river continue to convey?

STEP 2. Bridge-building

As a group, go back over the steps in the process. Recap what the river, salmon, and bear represent in us. How is this story our story? What does it say about the process of moving toward wholeness?

When people are ready, invite them to share.

STEPS 3–7

Steps 3–7 are the same as described on pages 108–9.

Session II (Part 1). Two Creation Stories

Preparation and Background for Step 1

This is a lengthy session, and you may want to plan more time for it.

If you asked the group members in Session I to bring in objects of nature, this session should begin with the participants sharing what they found and how they are like what they found.

The first story in this session is one that I heard some years ago and reconstructed out of my notes. It comes from Native Americans of Mexico. The names I gave the gods are simplified versions of names I have heard used. Put succinctly, this is my retelling of the story. The article on "Fire" in the IDB, vol. 2, pp. 268–69 is helpful in preparing to lead this session.

STEP 1. The Legend of the Proud God and the Scabby God

The leader reads the story aloud.

According to legend, there was a time when the sun and the moon were destroyed and the earth was plunged into darkness. This caused great distress among the people of the world, and their cries of distress reached the gods. So the gods gathered in a great council to decide what was to be done.

After much discussion, it was decided that a new sun and a new moon had to be created. To do this, one of the gods would be transformed into the sun god and another into the moon god. They then decided to ask for two volunteers who would cast themselves into a great fire and through this be transformed into the sun and the moon gods.

At first no one came forward. Then the proud god, Tecahu, came forward and said, "I will do it. I am not afraid. I am completely ready to do whatever is necessary to see that the

170

world is lighted by day. I will become the sun god." The other gods nodded in approval. But they still had no one for the moon. After much time had passed, Nanahu, an ugly, poor, scabby god, came forward. He was very afraid and he trembled at the thought of the fiery ordeal. But in his soul he had great compassion for the people of the world who were without light. After a brief consultation, the other gods decided that Nanahu would become the god who would light the world at night.

To prepare for their transformation, Tecahu, the proud god, and Nanahu, the ugly scabby god, were sent off to gather offerings to be put in the great fire. Each was to bring back four gifts: one to represent branches, one to represent hay, one to represent thorns, and one to serve as incense. Tecahu brought his gifts first. For branches, he brought exquisite feathers of rare birds; for hay, he brought strands of pure glistening gold; for thorns, he brought thorns of beautiful red coral; for incense, he brought the finest copal incense. The other gods were very pleased with these fine gifts.

Then Nanahu came with his gifts. Nanahu brought simple palm fronds for branches; reeds from the marshes for hay; for thorns, cactus thorns dipped in his own wounds; for incense, scabs taken from his own body. The other gods remarked to themselves that, however ugly Nanahu might be, it was clear that Nanahu's heart was pure and filled with compassion.

Then the time came for the transformation by fire. Tecahu, the proud god, moved rapidly forward and dashed for the great fire. But he stopped short. Was he afraid? Was his spirit not strong enough? He tried again. Again he failed. He tried a third time and failed again. And with a deep sense of shame he drew back, not daring to meet the stern gaze of the other gods.

Then Nanahu rose to his feet. His heart was filled with fear. He looked to the other gods as if to say "Give me strength. I'm not sure I can do it." Then he squared his shoulders and launched himself straight into the heart of the flames.

When Tecahu, the proud god, saw what Nanahu did he was overcome with shame, and he too cast himself into the flames.

As the fire subsided, two disks emerged, the first indescribably brilliant, the second pale but beautiful. And the gods, with humbled hearts, realized that Nanahu, the once scabby god, had now become the god of the sun and Tecahu, the once proud god, the god of the moon. And the people of the earth rejoiced that the light of life had returned.

1. Why do the gods act?
2. What does the sun do for life?
   - What does the moon do?
3. The sun and the moon rule (compare Genesis 1:16) what outer realities?
   - What inner realities do they represent?
4. In John 1:5 (RSV) it says, "The light shines in the darkness, and the darkness has not overcome it." How does that passage resonate with this story?
5. "One of the gods would be transformed"—what other words would one use for transformed?
   - What biblical words?
6. What does the "great fire" represent?
   - What are some of the biblical associations with fire?

In Justin, it says, "When Jesus went down into the water, fire was kindled in the Jordan."[11] See also Luke 3:16; 12:49–50.

   - Why is fire necessary in the transformation process?
7. Tecahu says he is not afraid. Does he have any fear at this point?
   - If so, what does he do with it?
   - How does that relate to what happens later?
   - To what voice is Tecahu listening?
8. What is your image of Nanahu?
   - What do the scabs indicate?
   - He has been what and he is what?
   - Who or what might have wounded him?
   - How does this relate to his compassion?
     See Isaiah 53:1–5.
9. Nanahu was afraid. Is he only afraid?
   - If not, where is his courage?
   - How does that relate to what happens later?
10. The gods decide that Tecahu is fit to illumine the day and Nanahu the night because of what?

11. Why go off and get gifts? What does that do for Tecahu and Nanahu?
12. How do you react to the gifts each brought?
13. Nanahu's heart was pure. How did they see that?
    - Where in the Bible does it talk about a pure heart?
    - What is a pure heart?
    - What makes it possible?
14. What keeps Tecahu from succeeding?
    - Why can he not do what he knew he could?
    - What does Tecahu learn about himself?
    - Who in the Gospels tried three times and failed?
    - How are they similar?
    - Where/how are "rocks" formed/transformed?
    - They are now solid because they were . . . ?
15. Nanahu acknowledges his fear and need of strength, but he acts. What do you make of this?
    - What resonates with this in the Gospel story?
16. What enabled Tecahu finally to act?
17. What do the gods learn?
18. What does Nanahu remember that will help him illumine the day?
19. What does Tecahu remember that will help him illumine the night?
20. What in the Gospel story resonates with the last section?
21. Why tell this story?
    - What is it about?

STEP 2. Bridge-building

Have the participants complete the sentences "I am like the gods/Tecahu/Nanahu in that I. . . ."

When people are ready, invite them to share.

STEPS 3–7

Steps 3–7 are the same as described on pages 108–9.

Session II (Part 2). Genesis 2:4—3:24
Preparation and Background

In using the creation story from Genesis 2, I have been selective in what parts I focused on. The story itself was written down several centuries before the story in Genesis 1—2:3. Each story has its own special truth it wants to convey, but it is not easy to hear it. In spite of the groundwork laid in Session I and the first half of this session, it is still a challenge for us to come to these stories in Genesis with a fresh and open mind. We need to keep the receiving Child alive in us to hear this message in a fresh way.

1. The setting of this story is a garden. What do we associate with a garden?
   - What is in a garden?
   - What is not in a garden?
2. What did God put in the garden?
   - Humans were originally intended to eat what?
     See Revelation 22:2: "endings" are like "beginnings."
3. What did God put in the middle (the heart) of the garden?
   - Why did God plant them both?
   - What do we expect in the middle of a garden?
   - What does this tell us about God?
   - Did God know what (s)he was doing?
4. The four rivers seem to be flowing outward from the center of the garden, so the water of life flows from where?
   - What do we associate with the number four?
5. What does "fourness" suggest?
     See IDB, vol. 3, p. 565.
6. If you were to say to a child, "There are all kinds of things in this room, but this one thing you are not to touch," what would that do for the child?
   - What is the child likely to do at some point?

7. What did God say about the trees?
   It will be helpful later to have a fix on the exact words.
8. Before eating of the tree of the knowledge of good and evil, does (hu)man know what good is?
   - Can you know what good is without knowing evil?
9. What would die if (hu)man ate of this tree?
10. Did God know what (s)he was doing in issuing this command?
11. What if God had put the knowledge-of-good-and-evil tree there and not told (hu)man about it?
12. It says "they were naked and not ashamed." What stage of life does this suggest?
13. What would it be like to be naked all the time?
14. What would be good about that? What would be not so good?
15. Who made the serpent and put it in the garden?
    - How is the serpent described?
    - What does "crafty" (NEB) or "subtle" (RSV) suggest?
    - What are some other words to describe this quality?
    - What does Jesus later suggest about us and serpents?
    - What does "wild" suggest?
    - Where else do we encounter wild creatures in the Bible?
    - Coming up to our time, where is a serpent used as a symbol?
    - What does it connote?
16. When the serpent asks about the tree, what is the response?
    - What is added to what God said before?
    - Where does this come from?
    - What does this tell us?

17. The serpent says, "You will not die." Is the serpent lying?
    - Was God lying?
    - Who is telling the truth?
    - If we are to find the truth, we have to listen to what?
18. Once they eat of the tree of the knowledge of good and evil, what can happen that could not have happened otherwise?
    - What have they lost?
    - What have they gained?
    - Is this a fall or a rise?
    - What point in the life cycle is like this?
    - What other points in the life cycle are similar?
    - What points in Jesus' life are like this?
19. As the humans leave the garden, what do they remember?
    - How might that be helpful to them?
    - What will be their core temptation?
20. The way back is guarded by flaming swords. If we were to go back, how would we have to go?
    - What would happen if we did not do this?
    - If we were to return, how would things be different?
21. What do we learn about God from this?
22. From now on, what is the task of human life?

STEP 2. Bridge-building

Have the participants paint, draw, sketch their conception of this story.

When people are ready, invite them to share.

STEPS 3–7

Steps 3–7 are the same as described on pages 108–9.

Session III. Genesis 32:22–31
Preparation and Background

This session is not as long as Session II. It is possible to carry over from Session II both sharing times (the second half of bridge-building from Session II, Parts 1 and 2), and the sharing of learnings from Parts 1 and 2 of Session II. You could also end Session II with the story of the proud god and the scabby god and hold the Genesis creation story over to this session.

In this session, we focus on a piece of the story of Jacob and Esau. This material has a clear kinship to the material we have been looking at so far. Jacob and Esau are, like Tecahu and Nanahu, prototypical humans. Jacob and Esau are twins who already struggle with each other before birth (Genesis 25:22). From birth, they incorporate opposite traits—Esau, hairy and wild, becoming a skillful hunter; Jacob, crafty and smooth, becoming a quiet homebody. From the beginning they are almost like a summary of the opposites that struggle within each human being as he or she moves through life. Each is attracted by what the other has, like the positive and negative poles of batteries. Jacob likes the game Esau brings home; Esau sells his birthright (as the firstborn) for the pottage Jacob prepared (Genesis 25:34). True to his name given at birth, Jacob (which means "he takes by the heel" [what he did to Esau during birth] or "he supplants" [what he did later]) tricks his aging and nearly blind father, Isaac, into giving him the patriarchal blessing. But he pays a price—he has to flee (leave the "tents" with which he was familiar). Jacob goes to his uncle Laban where he, in turn, is tricked by Laban. He works seven years to get Rebecca as his wife, only to be given her sister Leah; then he works another seven for Rebecca, a kind of protracted penance for his trickery against Esau and Isaac. Eventually the opposites have to be reunited, and Jacob, using his craftiness, leaves for his both longed for and dreaded enconter with Esau. But along the way he has another significant encounter. Birthing is rarely easy.

In preparing to lead this passage, read the chapters in Genesis (25—32:21) I summarized above. It helps to have the participants read the same material ahead of time, and to summarize the story at the beginning of Step 1 of this passage (Genesis 32:22–31). In addition, I recommend reading the articles in the IDB on "Esau" (vol. 2, pp. 125–26), on "Jacob" (vol. 2, pp. 782–86), and on "Thigh" (vol. 4, p. 630). The article on "Thigh" is especially important because it makes it clear not only where Jacob was wounded in this encounter but also what in Jacob was wounded.

STEP 1. Genesis 32:22–31

After going through the basic outline of the story of Jacob and Esau up to this point . . .

1. As Jacob is on his way back home to face Esau, what might he be thinking? feeling? wanting?
2. What is at stake in his return home?
3. What does he expect might happen? Why?
4. What kind of people are Jacob and Esau?
   - If Jacob and Esau were different parts of the same person, how would you describe what has happened up to this point?
   - What has not yet happened?
   - What would be the best possible outcome?
   - What might it take for that to happen?
5. In the opening of this part of the story, Jacob sends everybody ahead across the stream and he stays behind all alone . . . at night . . . beside the stream . . . in the middle of barren country. What is your sensory impression of this place?
   - What would you hear, smell, touch, see, taste?

- What feelings does it evoke?
- Of what does it remind you?
- Why would Jacob choose to remain alone in this setting?
- What did he want?
- What did he expect?

6. A human-like figure comes and wrestles with Jacob in the night. Why does this figure come at this time in this setting?
   - What internal need in Jacob evokes this figure?
   - With what is Jacob wrestling?
   - What does the figure want?

7. The figure does not prevail and wounds Jacob in the thigh. What does the thigh represent in Jacob?
   - Why is he wounded there?
   - What is there about nighttime encounters in general that makes them seem to wound us?
   - What comes out in these times that does not come out at other times?

8. Why does the figure have to leave?

9. What if night figures populated our waking/conscious time?

10. Why won't Jacob let the figure go?
    - What does this suggest about what it takes to receive blessing from the figures of the night?

11. Why does the figure ask Jacob's name?
    - What does asking this question do for Jacob?
    - It mobilizes what part of Jacob?

12. What does this suggest about the connections that have to be made for nighttime encounters to yield blessing?
    - If this does not happen, what then?

13. Up till now, Jacob has been "the supplanter" (the interpretation of the name Jacob). Now he is to be known as the one who strives/wrestles with God (Israel). What has happened?

- Does he lose his previous identity (name) altogether?
- If not, what has been changed in that?
- What does his new identity add to the old one?
- How will this affect his confrontation with Esau?
- If *he* is Israel, *what* is Israel?

14. Jacob encountered God where?
    - What does this suggest about God?
15. Why is there no name given in response to Jacob's request? (Jacob still has his "old" name.)
16. Jacob has seen *God* face-to-face. When did that become clear?
    - What might he have thought before that?
17. He leaves limping from his wound. What will this do for him in the future?
18. He leaves with another name. What will this do for him later?
19. What does this story say about God?
20. What does it say about the human relationship to God?

STEP 2. Bridge-building

For this exercise I have put together a guided meditation based on the story.[12] I also had a recording of a brook, which I put on when people were ready for the meditation itself.[13] If you think the group members would not want to lie down directly on the floor of your meeting room, you can ask them to bring large towels to the session.

To get the participants ready for the meditation, explain what is to come: They are going to be talked through the story as if each person were in Jacob's place (but with their own identities and names). To get started, have the group members spread out, lie down on the floor, close their eyes, and relax. Have them do some deep breathing, focusing on the breathing itself, on the cool air as they inhale, the warm air as they exhale. Have them shift their awareness to various parts of their bodies. If there are any tense places, tense them up even more and then let go. By now the group should be ready to go with you through the rest. Be sure to go slowly, leaving pauses for the participants to imagine the various steps. You can start the stream record now if you have one. (Using the recording helps considerably in getting into this.)

1. Keeping your eyes closed, imagine that you are all alone in a very barren, mountainous country, by a river, at night. It is very dark. There are no lights anywhere except the stars. The main sound you hear is the sound of the river.
2. A strange figure comes on you there in the dark, and you wrestle with that figure in the darkness.
3. After a long time passes in struggle, the figure wounds you. Where is that wounded place in you?
4. The figure wants to go, but you will not let it, and you say to it, "I will not let you go until you bless me!" Say that to the figure now in your imagination.
5. The figure asks you your name. Say your first name to the figure. Now the figure says you will be getting a new name to add to your old name. Listen for what new name you might receive right now. What might that new name mean for you?
6. Now slowly open your eyes, and in silence where you are, take time to reflect on this experience and to jot down some notes about it for the wrap-up session. If it was difficult for you to get into the experience, or some part of it, spend some time reflecting on that. If you were able to get into it, reflect on what happened. (In either case, it is important to maintain the silence so that each person can digest this in his or her own way.)

The reminder about the ground rule of silence seems to be needed, because the natural thing at this point is to talk. This

*needs to be resisted so the bridging inward can be completed. I
imagine that Jacob might well have never had this encounter had
he kept people with him that night and stayed up and talked.
Silence helps us gain access to the unconscious.*

STEPS 3–7

Steps 3–7 are the same as described on pages 108–9.

Session IV. G.P. ¶188, Mark 10:13–16 (and parallels); G.P. ¶101 and 102, Matthew 13:44–48; G.P. ¶97, Mark 4:30–32; Luke 11:2–4

Preparation

In preparation for this session, read the section on the
kingdom of God in Norman Perrin's *Rediscovering the
Teaching of Jesus;*[14] the chapter on the same subject in my
Questions Are the Answer;[15] and John Sanford's *The
Kingdom Within*[16] if you have not yet done so.

This session begins with another look at Mark 10:13–
16. Then there is a series of short texts on the kingdom.
There are no bridging exercises for these. As we go along,
however, there are some bridging questions. At the end,
there is a bridge-building exercise intended to draw on
the energy of the whole session. Someone should read
each text aloud before you start.

STEP 1A. Mark 10:13–16 (and parallels)

*This key passage is intentionally repeated here as a means of
review. Some new questions are added for the focus of this session.*

1. Who are "they" that bring the children?
   • What do they want?
2. Why is *touch* important?
3. What stands in their way?
4. What hooks the disciples to incline them to act this
   way?

5. What does this suggest about the obstacles on the path toward the source of healing?
6. What part of ourselves do we have to deal with?
7. Jesus is furious. At what is his anger directed?
8. So far, we have four roles: "they," the children, the disciples, and Jesus. Thinking of these as parts of yourselves, how are you like each of them? Reflect for a minute. Which is the least used part of you?
    ● Which part is the most used?
    ● What would it look like if you changed things around?
    ● What would it take for that change to occur?
9. "To such" belongs the kingdom. . . . What does that mean?
    ● What would it take for us to strengthen the Child part of us (and soften the hindering part)?
10. The Child in us is the receiver of the kingdom. What might that involve?
11. The "whoever" in us is then to enter the kingdom. What might that involve?

STEP 1B. Matthew 13:44, 13:45–46, 13:47–48

Matthew 13:44
1. What is the man doing when he finds the treasure?
    ● Where is the treasure?
    ● What might the field represent?
2. Why does he not just take the treasure and go?
    ● What might the whole field represent?
    ● He hid the treasure again temporarily. What does this suggest?
3. He had to sell *all* that he had. What might it mean to sell all?
    ● What might "all" represent?
    ● How did he come by "all" he had?
    ● Up to the moment of finding the treasure, what

would he have thought about it? felt toward it? wanted to do with it?
- How has finding the treasure altered what he thought? felt? wanted?
- What part of the man received the treasure?
- What part of him acted?
4. What does this parable say about the kingdom?
5. If we were to reconstruct the process so we could see what it would take for us to go through it, what would be the steps?

E.g., first plowing under the surface of the ground; second, recognizing the buried treasure, etc.

Matthew 13:45–46

1. Who or what is the searching merchant?
   - And the fine pearls are what?
2. How have we seen the kingdom searching for people in previous sessions?
3. How are pearls formed?
   - What stimulates them to grow?
   - Where are they found?
   - What does this suggest?
4. What would it take for us to become pearls of great value?
   - If we do not do that, what might happen?

Matthew 13:47–48

Verses 49–50 are probably later commentary.

1. What might the sea symbolize?
   - The net? The fish?
2. This is the second time we have seen the kingdom as active. What in us might the net be thrown into?
   - What would we have to do to allow that to happen (receive it)?
3. At what point is it possible to discriminate what is good and bad?
   - When would we like to be able to discriminate?

- So in order for the net to work we have to . . .?
4. How is this like discovering the hidden treasure?

STEP 1C. Mark 4:30–32

1. This parable seems to suggest patience: The kingdom may start small, but it ends big, so don't give up. But what if we look at the process? What does the mustard seed go through on its journey of becoming?
   - What if our growth were to parallel that journey?
2. The seed is first sown. What might sow us?
3. Then comes a period under the ground. What does it feel like there?
4. What has to happen to the seed for its inner potential to be released?
5. What does that moment feel like?
6. What does that say about us?
7. As the new plant starts to push toward the surface, what does it have to believe?
   - What does that say to us?
   - What else is growing at the same time?
   - What does that suggest?
8. As it pushes through the soil, what might that feel like?
9. What comes next during its first period of growth?
   - What does that say about us?
10. When it becomes mature, what happens then?
    - What does this say about the goal of growth?
11. What will happen if that is not mentioned?
    - What does this say?
12. Taking all four passages together, what do we know now about the kingdom?

STEP 1D. Luke 11:2–4

This is Luke's version of the Lord's Prayer. It is probably closer to what Jesus taught than Matthew's version. I put it here to put some fresh content into it so it can be used as a resource for a guided meditation. When the word Father is used, the word *abba** probably resonates with it, because what follows is a series of command forms. The first two are the passive command form, as if I were to say, "May the door be shut by you!" To release the intention of the first two sections, I put them in direct command form like the rest.

1. When a child addresses a parent as "Father" or "Mother," what is it trying to do?
   - What does that say about the intention of the word here?
2. "Honor your name" or "Get your name honored!" How can God's name be dishonored?
   - Who might dishonor it?
   - Why does God let it happen?
   - What does this request imply?
   - Through whom might increased honoring occur?
3. "Bring in your kingdom!" Why wouldn't God want to do this?
   - Can we change God's mind?
   - Why does God need us to do this reminding?
   - Through whom might the kingdom come?
4. "Do your will." or "Get your will done." What part of God is this intended to awaken?
   - What stands in the way of God's will?
   - How can these obstacles be removed?
5. "Do it here, not just up there!" What does that add?
6. "Give us today's bread (only?)." What does bread represent?
   - Why the focus on today?
   - What needs to be fed in us?
   - What if we got a lot of food all at once (and were fed it)?
   - What does that suggest?

Indebtedness and sin were synonymous. To keep it consistent, I put "sin" (or "debts") in both halves of this next command. "Forgive us our sins because we ourselves forgive everyone who sins against us."

---

*See the discussion of the word *abba* in Chapter V, p. 131.

7. Luke has a challenging version of this sentence. God is "commanded" to forgive us because of what?
   - What if we didn't do our part?
   - Who needs to be forgiven?
   - What would be some other words for forgiveness?
   - Where have we seen forgiveness at work in previous sessions?
   - Forgiveness is the process whereby. . . ?
8. "Do not lead us into temptation." Where have we seen temptation at work?
   - How else might we get into temptation?
   - What might this sentence imply?

STEP 2. Bridge-building

Have the group spread out a bit and get in comfortable positions. If they are sitting, have them get both feet on the floor (to get grounded). If they want to lie down on the floor on their backs for this, that is fine too. Have the participants close their eyes and do some deep breathing and a body check, as in the Jacob session (pp. 180–81). Then ask them to track their awareness—thoughts/feelings/wants—as you read slowly, phrase by phrase, with pauses between phrases, through the Lord's Prayer as it is found in Luke. In doing this, you may want to follow the suggestions in Step 1 or read it from a translation such as the *Revised Standard Version*. After this, have the group members write up their own paraphrases of this prayer.

When people are ready, invite them to share.

STEPS 3–7

Steps 3–7 are the same as described on pages 108–9.

Session V

Preparation

This session has no new texts. During the first part, have the group members review what they have done in the first four sessions, including the stories and texts, the bridging exercises, the wants, and the learnings. Then ask them to go through Steps 3–6 in the following way (for Steps 3 and 4, ask people to write their answers to the following questions):

1. What kind of a person do I want to be five years hence? What kind of family and/or other group do I want to be part of? What kind of society? (These questions are intended to personalize the kingdom of God.)
2. What have I learned here that will help me move toward what I said I wanted?
3. What do I want to do in the next week to start me on that journey?

Do Steps 5 and 6 as usual.

After everyone has done this, done the evaluations, and taken a break, you are ready for worship as suggested in the previous sequences.

CHAPTER VIII

Fourth Sequence:
Getting at the Christian Story Inside Us

The last decisive turning point in [Jesus'] life is the resolution to go to Jerusalem with his disciples in order to confront people there with his message in the face of the coming Kingdom of God.

—Günther Bornkamm[1]

I came to cast fire upon the earth; and would that it were already kindled! I have a baptism to be baptized with; and how I am constrained until it is accomplished!

—Luke 12:49–50, RSV

O Jerusalem, Jerusalem, . . . how often would I have gathered your children together as a hen gathers her brood under her wings, and you would not!

—Luke 13:34, RSV

Though they could charge him with nothing deserving death, yet they asked Pilate to have him killed. . . . But God raised him from the dead. . . . We bring you the good news that what God promised to the fathers, this [God] has fulfilled to us their children by raising Jesus; as also it is written in the second psalm, "Thou art my Son, today I have begotten thee."

—Acts 13:28, 30, 32–33, RSV

This final sequence covers the time from Jesus' decision to go to Jerusalem for the last time(s) through the beginnings of the resurrection. I have chosen to focus on what seem to be major points of becoming in the final act of the drama of Jesus' life. In this drama, Peter played a major role. In a way, Jesus and Peter both go through a baptism by fire, much like Nanahu and Tecahu. Tecahu and Peter were both convinced that their strength would carry them through—only to discover their weakness the hard way. And Jesus, while acting more forcefully than Nanahu at the outset, by moving into the darkness of the garden and the pain of the cross, seems to pave the way for the light of the resurrection which followed.

In attempting to listen actively to these texts, many things are apt to deafen us. For one thing, we have heard the story so often that we think we know what is coming. This knowledge comes in part from the Gospels themselves, but the Gospels have been colored by the impact of the resurrection and the natural tendency of projection at which we looked earlier. The certainty of hindsight became the certainty of foresight. However, one of the most freeing results of historical-critical work on the Gospels has been that Jesus himself did not, in all likelihood, know in advance what was to come—an uncertainty that, given the reality of human freedom and capacity to choose, even God shared. So the way to come to these texts is with an open mind, ready to discover the real human journey of becoming that Jesus and his followers went through in their baptism by fire.

Another principal obstacle to hearing these texts is the lack of an accurate mental image of the setting, especially the setting in Jerusalem. For me, many things fell dramatically into place when I visited Jerusalem a few years ago. The temple area that Jesus cleansed, for example, which was called at that time "the court of the gentiles" (and was originally intended as a place for gentiles to be able to worship), is much larger than I had imagined. Four football fields would easily fit into the main parts of that area. By contrast, the Kidron valley, which is between the east wall of the temple and the Mount of Olives, is much shallower and narrower than I had imagined. The probable site of Gethsemane is about a thousand feet from the east wall of the temple, and the top of the Mount of Olives is about two thousand feet from that same wall. To imagine the last days of Jesus' life in a way that would enable the narratives about these days to come alive, it helps to have an accurate mental picture of the setting (see IDB, vol. 2, pp. 843–66).

One more aspect is vitally important: knowing something about the cultural, political, religious, and economic situation of Jerusalem in Jesus' day. The most helpful single resource I know for this is Joachim Jeremias' *Jerusalem in the Time of Jesus*, now available in paperback.[2] For instance, Jeremias makes it clear how central the temple was to the economy of Jerusalem. Jerusalem had about 25,000 people in Jesus' day, and up to 18,000 people alone were employed in building the temple. Eighty-two women were employed full-time just to produce two curtains (30′ × 60′) for the temple each year.[3] In addition, the other principal source of income and employment came from the pilgrim traffic. The Jewish pilgrims, who were required to come to Jerusalem for three festivals a year, were also supposed to spend one-tenth of their annual income in Jerusalem itself. Without the temple and the commerce associated with it, Jerusalem would have dwindled rapidly to a small, insignificant village. On top of this, there was a good deal of economic exploitation centered in the temple. The doves or pigeons, for example, which were the least offering one could present and which had to be purchased in Jerusalem with Jerusalem currency (which also had to be purchased), often went for up to ten times the price charged elsewhere.[4] Much of this trading was done within the temple area itself. From this mere sampling of information about the temple, one can begin to appreciate the magnitude of Jesus' challenge. Like the great prophets who went before him, he was calling on the whole establishment to repent.

Session I. G.P. ¶160, Luke 12:49–50; G.P. ¶211, Luke 13:34; G.P. ¶122, Mark 8:27–33 (and parallels)

Preparation and Background for Step 1

In this session, we focus on Jesus as he turns toward Jerusalem. His decision to do so is lost in the mists of time. My hunch is that he had discovered that moving toward wholeness involves more than individual healing. At some point, the powers in the world which constrain us in our movement toward wholeness must be challenged to change. For the world of Jesus, Jerusalem represented not just where God was thought to dwell in an especially powerful way but also where the access to God was blocked or impeded.

STEP 1A. G.P. ¶160, Luke 12:49–50

1. Focusing first on the image of fire—what does this image suggest?
   - Where in the Old Testament is fire encountered?
   - What prophetic figure is associated with fire especially?

"Elijah" means "Yahweh is El" or "Yahweh is God."

2. In verse 49, what feelings . . . thoughts . . . wants . . . might Jesus have had as he said this?
3. In terms of traditional male and female roles, with which one might this kind of action be associated?
4. In verse 50, Jesus speaks of a future baptism. To what might he be referring?
   - What might this baptism be like?
5. The word translated "constrained" means more liter-

ally "pressed down" or "pressed together." What feelings are conveyed by this verb?

6. In the birthing process, of what part is this reminiscent?
   - What might that suggest?
7. If we add in verse 51, what else does this say about what Jesus and/or others might have thought?
   - What seems to lie ahead?

STEP 1B. G.P. ¶211, Luke 13:34

1. Reading verse 34, for what had Jesus hoped?
   - What feelings go with this?
   - What is Jesus thinking? feeling? wanting?
2. In terms of traditional male and female roles, with which role would this be associated?
3. Putting this together with the preceding text, what does this say about Jesus?
4. Adding verse 35a, what does Jesus foresee as possible?
   - What else could happen?

STEP 1C. G.P. ¶122, Mark 8:27–33 (and parallels)

Caesarea Philippi is the northernmost point mentioned to which Jesus went. It is on a plateau overlooking the north end of the Jordan River valley, the setting for most of Jesus' ministry up to this point. To the northwest is Mount Hermon.

1. As we pick up the story in Mark, Jesus has just been in Bethsaida on the north end of the Sea of Galilee. He is now in Caesarea Philippi, some twenty miles to the north. If he is thinking about going to Jerusalem, why might he have gone here?
   - With what issues might he be wrestling?
   - Luke drops the setting. Why?
2. "Who do people say that I am?" What does this question presuppose?
   - Why does Jesus ask?
3. Looking at the replies, what do we know about John the Baptist?

- What have they seen in Jesus that would lead them to say this?
4. "Others say Elijah." What do we know about Elijah?
    - What have people seen in Jesus that would lead them to say this?
    - What do John and Elijah have in common?
    - How was Jesus different from these two?
5. "Others say one of the prophets." For Jesus to be any of these, what would have to have happened?
    - What does this say about how people are seeing Jesus?
    - From whence is this picture coming?
    - Matthew adds "Jeremiah." Why?
6. How does Jesus react to this feedback?
    - Why does he not say no to it?
7. Jesus asks them again, but Peter responds. What does this say about Peter's role?
8. Peter answers, "You are the Christ (Messiah)." What do we know about the Messiah?
    - Who is this figure?
    - What would this person be expected to do?
    - What would this person not be expected to do?
    - Why do people long for messiahs? I need a messiah because the world is . . . and I am. . . .
    - What word in today's language would convey the "Messiah" idea?
9. Compare Peter's answer in Matthew and Luke. What do they add?
    - What does this tell us about the tendency of the tradition?
    - In the tradition, Jesus becomes what?
    - If we are to reverse the tradition, we have to do what?
10. Skipping Matthew's insertion, Jesus' immediate reaction is to "charge" them. Given the fact that Peter responded, Jesus thinks what?
    - The word translated "charge" is the same word

translated "rebuke" in verse 32. The feelings that go with this word might be what?
- Why does Jesus rebuke them?
- How does this contrast to his response to the previous feedback?
- What is wrong with being seen as the Messiah?
- From whence did the "messiah" idea come?
- What does this suggest about how Jesus might see himself?
- He wants them to keep the messiah idea to themselves. Why?
11. Going back briefly to Matthew's insertion, how does Jesus respond there?
    - How does that differ?
    - From what period of time might this have come?
12. Returning to Mark 8:31, what might the "Son of man" mean?
    - Why might Jesus have spoken this way?
13. The chief priests are where? (Compare Matthew 16:21.)
    - What might Jesus have wanted in going to Jerusalem?
    - In the wilderness, when Jesus saw the temple, what was he unwilling to do?
    - What is happening now?
14. "Be killed and after three days rise." What does that sound like?
    - At what point in time was that clear?
    - From what period would this seem to come then?
15. What might Jesus have actually said?
16. Peter now "rebukes" Jesus (same verb as in verse 30). To what is Peter objecting?
    - How does that relate to what he said to Jesus before?

The word translated "suffer" [v. 31], means to have things happen to you, as opposed to *making* things happen.

17. Jesus again "rebukes" Peter. Why are such strong feelings coursing through this passage?
    - We have met Satan before where?
    - What did Satan do for Jesus then?
    - What is the temptation now?
    - What is Peter/Satan doing for Jesus here?
18. You are not on God's side. To whom does the you refer?
19. Luke leaves out this last part. Why?
20. What issues are left for Jesus as he leaves this experience?
    - For Peter and the disciples?

STEP 2. Bridge-building

For this exercise, invite the participants to ask themselves the following questions and write their answers down in silence:

What is your Jerusalem?

What do people say about you?

What do you say about yourself?

What does your masculine side say about your Jerusalem?

What does your feminine side say about your Jerusalem?

When people are ready, invite them to share.

STEPS 3–7

Steps 3–7 are the same as described on pages 108–9.

Session II. G.P. ¶196, Mark 11:1–10 (and parallels); G.P. ¶198, Mark 11:11 (and parallels); G.P. ¶199, Mark 11:12–14 (and parallels); G.P. ¶200, Mark 11:15–19 (and parallels)

Preparation and Background for Step 1

In Appendix II there is a reprint of an article I wrote for *Youth* magazine on the subject of this session. The style of the article reflects the intended readership, but it contains some background information that will be useful in preparing to lead this session. Jeremias' *Jerusalem in the Time of Jesus*, mentioned previously, is especially significant in understanding the scope of Jesus' challenge. It is the scope of his challenge which is the major reason, as I understand it, that he was crucified.

STEP 1A. G.P. ¶196, Mark 11:1–10 (and parallels)

1. From the Mount of Olives, the city of Jerusalem can be seen across the narrow depression called the Kidron valley. In the foreground is the east wall of the temple. What did Jerusalem represent for people of Jesus' time?
   - What was the economic, political, social, and religious significance of the temple?
   - When would Jesus have been here before?
   - As Jesus and his disciples looked across at the temple, what might they have been thinking? feeling? wanting?
2. If someone sent you for a "colt," with what would you return?
   - "On which no one has ever sat"—what does this suggest?
   - Why would Jesus want this kind of animal?
   - Matthew changes Mark. What change is made? Why?
   - How does this alter the story?
3. Knowing Jesus' aversion to titles, to whom does "the Lord" refer?
   - What has to have happened previously for this signal to work?
   - How does Jesus know the animal that he wants will be there?

As leader, you may want to comment, as a transition, on the festival[s] when people used leafy branches, etc. See Appendix II.

4. In Mark, verse 9, it says they shouted "Hosanna!" Hosanna means "God save us." From what might people have wanted God to save them?
   - For them, who was the enemy?
   - What had Jesus previously said about enemies?
5. In Mark, verse 9, who might be the "he" that comes?
   - How do Matthew and Luke change that?
   - What does that do?
6. In Mark, verse 10, what is it that is coming?
   - What does this say about people's hopes?
   - How is this verse changed in Matthew and Luke?
   - What is the impact of the change?

STEP 1B. G.P. ¶198, Mark 11:11 (and parallels)

1. In Mark, what does Jesus do?
   - What does he not do? Why?
   - Matthew and Luke eliminate this step. Why?

STEP 1C. G.P. ¶199, Mark 11:12–14 (and parallels)

1. In verse 12 it says Jesus was . . . ?
2. What does he do when he sees the fig tree?
3. What does this tell us about the mood of Jesus?
4. Matthew leaves out what part of Mark's story? Why?
5. Luke leaves it out altogether. Why?

STEP 1D. G.P. ¶200, Mark 11:15–19 (and parallels)

1. In verses 15 and 16 in Mark, Jesus does what four things?
   - What does each of these represent?
   - How could he have done this?
   - Matthew and Luke leave out parts of what Mark says Jesus did. Why?
   - If the temple authorities had heeded Jesus' challenge, what would have happened to the temple? to Jerusalem?

2. In verse 17, what does it say Jesus wanted to happen in this area of the temple?
   - What would have to happen for this to be possible?
3. What do Matthew and Luke leave out?
4. Who does "all the nations" include?
5. What does Jesus hope might happen?
   - How does this relate to his previous activities in Galilee?
6. Given the political situation of the time, the Jewish authorities might have said, "The problem with our world is . . ."
   - What does this action indicate about where Jesus sees the problem?
   - If there is an enemy, who is it?
7. Throughout this narrative, what have been the feelings, thoughts, and wants of the disciples?
   - Of the temple authorities?
   - Of others in the temple area?
   - Of Jesus?
8. What does Jesus not do?
   - Jesus' action was akin to what kind of action(s) in our time?

STEP 2. Bridge-building

For the first part of this exercise, ask the participants to draw or sketch or paint the scene of the cleansing of the temple. Then invite them to turn the picture over, or take another piece of paper, and address the following questions: "If Jesus were to clear out the cluttered part of me, what would he clear?" "How can I tap into that Power to allow that to happen?"

When people are ready, invite them to share.

STEPS 3–7

Steps 3–7 are the same as described on pages 108–9.

Session III. G.P. ¶237c, Luke 22:31–34; G.P. ¶239, Mark 14:32–42 (and parallels); G.P. ¶241, Luke 22:54–62

Preparation for Step 1

For this session, the bridge-building comes first, so Step 1 this time is similar to other Step 2s, and vice versa. The purpose of this is to provide people with an experience that will help them be able to listen to one of the key issues raised in the texts, the issue of projection. Projections are notoriously difficult to get at, so it is important to do this exercise with as little explanation as possible and to take people through it as outlined. In the first part of the exercise, people may come up with things that seem frivolous, but the things that people come up with are generally significant, and "re-owning" them in the second part of the exercise can be a healing, though unsettling, experience. Do the exercise yourself a step at a time to get a feel for how it goes.

STEP 1

For this exercise, have the group divide up into pairs. Then have each person take a sheet of paper and fold it in half vertically or draw a line down the center. Next, have them finish the following sentences quickly, without censoring or editing. Read them one by one, giving participants a short time to finish each one.

1. I am not. . . .
2. I would never. . . .
3. I do not like people who. . . .
4. What I most dislike about my mother and/or father is (was). . . .

Next have them share with one another what they have written, just as they wrote it, with no editing, no explanation, no justification—just rapidly share. (They may always pass on an item if they choose.) On the other half of the sheet, have them complete the following sentences opposite the corresponding numbers that appear on the other side.

1. I am (what I said I was not) in that.... (More than one sentence, if they had more than one response written under number one.)
2. I have or I could (what I said I would never) in that I....
3. I didn't like myself when I did what I don't like in others.
4. I acted like my mother or father when I....

Then have the participants share with one another what they have discovered.

STEP 2A. G.P. ¶237c, Luke 22:31–34

1. Where have we encountered Satan before?
   - What do you make of this conversing between Jesus and Satan?
   - Of what is this reminiscent?
   - What right does Satan have to demand?
   - The you in verse 31 is plural. Who does Peter represent?
   - Who else has been sifted like wheat? Why?
   - What falls away when wheat is sifted, and what is kept?
   - What in Peter needs to fall away?
2. "That your faith may not fail"—does Peter's faith fail?
   - Why does Peter have to go through this?
   - How will this enhance his ability to strengthen others?
3. "Lord, I am ready ...."—how can he say that?
   - Who is saying it?
   - In the wheat analogy, what part is speaking?
4. "You will deny me"—what does Jesus know about Peter that Peter does not?

- Peter's name means rock. To become a rock, Peter has to what?

STEP 2B. G.P. ¶239, Mark 14:32–39

We do not know for sure where Gethsemane was exactly, but the likely place is just across the Kidron valley on the lower part of the Mount of Olives. Jesus and his disciples would have gone through this general area on their way into the city of Jerusalem, and from this location, one can look up at the gate of the city through which they would have gone.

1. Jesus takes along Peter, James, and John. Where have we seen these three before?
   - Why does Jesus take them along?
2. Jesus begins to be greatly distressed (a word which in Greek conveys a sense of awe) and troubled. What is leading Jesus to feel this way?
   - What had he hoped?
   - What has happened?
3. In verse 34, the word soul is *psyche* in Greek, and the word translated "sorrowful" is the one used for grieving. What has Jesus lost?
   - What in Jesus is dying?
   - What does he want from his disciples?
   - The word watch means to "stay awake." How else would you describe what Jesus wants?
   - Why is this important?
4. What does verse 35 say Jesus wants from God?
   - What does he think God can do?
5. In verse 36, Jesus addresses God as "Abba" and says, "All things are possible for you." Who in Jesus is speaking?
   - Are all things possible for God?
   - What might God not be able (or want) to do?
6. What possibilities are there at this point? What else?
7. He next says, "Remove this cup from me." What is a cup like?
   - How is a cup different from a flask or bottle?

- What can be poured into a cup?
- What does Jesus think is being poured into his cup?[5]
- Why does he want it removed?
- If death is being poured in, what would be lost?
- What might be gained?

8. The next phrase says in Greek "but not what I want, but what you . . ." The sentence is incomplete. The translators fill in the blank with the word want (wilt). How would you fill it in?
   - What might God want?
   - What is Jesus discovering in these moments?
   - What is God learning?
   - If God is like a parent, how is God parent-like here?
9. In verse 37, Jesus finds them sleeping, but Peter is the one addressed. Why?
   - What is pushing them to sleep?
10. The process is repeated three times. What does that tell us about the nature of this time for Jesus?
    - For the disciples?

STEP 2C. G.P. ¶241, Luke 22:54–62

1. Peter alone follows Jesus, at a distance. What does this say about Peter?
   - Peter wants what?
2. Peter denies Jesus three times. Out of what part of Peter does this action come?
   - What "possesses" him?
3. He finally remembers what Jesus said. What blocked his memory up to this point?
4. He goes out and weeps bitterly. What is Peter thinking? feeling? wanting?
   - What is he doing?
   - What part of Peter is being born?

5. What has happened to his faith, which Jesus mentioned earlier?
6. How has this experience sifted him to be able to strengthen others?
7. What does this say about the roots of compassion?
8. How do these texts fit with what we did in the beginning of this session?

When people are ready, invite them to share.

STEPS 3–7

Steps 3–7 are the same as described on pages 108–9.

Session IV. G.P. ¶241, Luke 22:67, 70–71; G.P. ¶244, Mark 15:2–5 (and parallels); G.P. ¶249, Mark 15:22–32 (and parallels); G.P. ¶250, Mark 15:33–41 (and parallels)

Preparation and Background

In this session, we will be looking at only part of the various accounts of the trial. Previously, when Jesus was asked about himself, he would not answer directly. The passages we will be looking at are consistent with that and reflect what might have happened.

STEP 1A. G.P. ¶241, Luke 22:67, 70–71

1. In verse 67a, Jesus is spoken to: "If you are the Christ, tell us." From whom does the "Christ" idea come?
   - If Jesus were to say, "Yes, I am," what would be the consequences?
   - If he were to say, "No, I am not," what would be the consequences?
   - What does this sound like?
   - When has Jesus confronted a similar situation?
   - What does this tell us about the value of that previous experience?

- What are Jesus, his interrogator, and God thinking? feeling? wanting?
2. In 67b and 68 we hear Jesus' answer. What does this answer do?
   - To what is it similar?
   - What can we learn from his response about how to deal with similar situations?
3. In verse 70 the question is what?
   - Whose idea is this?
   - Jesus' response is, "You say that I am," but Jesus might have said (to himself) "I am (what)?"
4. In verse 71 they say they have heard *it*. What have they heard?
5. Going back briefly to verse 69, does it seem to match the other verses at which we have looked?
   - If not, what are the options?
   - What seems most likely?

STEP 1B. G.P. ¶244, Mark 15:2–5 (and parallels)

1. We now turn to the trial before Pilate. What does Pilate ask?
   - From where does that idea come?
   - What are Jesus' options in responding?
2. Jesus' answer is what?
   - What does he mean by that?
   - How would you put his reply in your own words?
3. Turning to Matthew 27:14, what does he add?
4. We have looked at two traditions about the trial, which agree that he gave "no answer" answers. Others have him giving various answers. What seems more likely?

STEP 1C. G.P. ¶249, Mark 15:22–32 (and parallels)

1. As Jesus was brought to Golgotha, what might have been his feelings? thoughts? wants?
   - What about the absent disciples? the criminals

who were crucified with him? the authorities? God?

2. Why might he have refused the wine with myrrh?

The third hour would be 9:00 A.M.

3. Crucifixion involved being nailed hand and foot to the beams of the cross, being tied to the cross with ropes, and stripped of clothing. What feelings . . . thoughts . . . wants . . . might Jesus have had at this point?

4. The charge against him read, "The King of the Jews." What might Jesus have thought about that, given what we've been looking at in previous sessions?

5. Did Jesus want to destroy the temple?
   - What did he want to destroy?
   - What might he have hoped to rebuild in three days?

6. "He saved others"—did he save others?
   - What did he mean by saving?
   - What did he say saved others?
   - What might he have hoped would save him?

STEP 1D. G.P. ¶250, Mark 15:33–41 (and parallels)

The sixth hour would have been noon, the ninth hour would be 3 P.M.

1. What do the three hours of darkness suggest?
   - This is for Jesus _____, for the disciples _____, for God _____?

2. In verse 34 the word *Eloi* goes back to a Hebrew root meaning "power." Why might Jesus have used this name for God at this point?

3. The verb translated "forsaken" can also be translated "left behind," "abandoned," "deserted," or "allowed to remain." What word would reflect your understanding of this moment? Why?

4. If the *El* part of God is absent, what other part of God might still be there?

206

- How might this relate to Peter's struggle?
5. What is Jesus *not* saying that God has done?
6. What is happening to Jesus' understanding of God at this moment?
7. The Gospel of John has as Jesus' last words "It is finished." What is finished at the point of Jesus' death?
    - What is not finished?
    - What is dying?
    - What is being born?
8. The temple curtain is torn in two (ripped open) at this moment. What was thought to be behind the curtain?
    - What is exposed?
    - How does this relate to Jesus' exposure on the cross?
    - What does this recall from the baptism?
    - Who saw God then?
    - Who sees God now?
    - What might people have expected to see?
    - What would they actually have seen?
    - When did God start hiding?
    - How does what is happening now relate to that?
9. The centurion says, "Truly this man was *a* son of God." To what is he responding?
    - What is the difference between *the* and *a* son of God?
10. In verse 40 we hear about some friendly witnesses. Why were they here while the others were not?

STEP 2. Bridge-building

Invite the participants to paint or draw or sketch the scene of the crucifixion in three tiers—with God or a symbol of God in the top tier, the crucifixion itself in the middle tier, and the absent significant others in the bottom tier. Then invite them to put themselves into the picture.

When people are ready, invite them to share.

STEPS 3–7

Steps 3–7 are the same as described on pages 108–9.

Session V. Luke 24:13–35

Preparation

I have put the text (Luke 24:13–35) into the first part of Session V because of the nature of the sequence. It is difficult to go in a single session from crucifixion to resurrection. The intent in the first part of this session is to explore the part of the resurrection that happens within the lives of the disciples—what the resurrection process looks like in their experience.

STEP 1. Luke 24:13–35

Before going into this passage, it helps to review what has happened to the disciples, starting from the very beginning. They were working at their jobs as fishermen, etc., when they. . . . And then they. . . , etc. The most recent thing that happened is what?

1. What do we know about the grieving process?
    - What feelings . . . thoughts . . . wants . . . are a part of it?
    - How long does it generally take?
    - How do you know when you've made it through?
    - Do you ever make it all the way through?
    - What does that tell us about how the resurrection took place in the disciples' lives?
2. As the disciples walk toward Emmaus, Jesus appears with them. In what form?
    - How might we describe this if it happened today?

3. Their eyes were "kept." What blinded them?

The verb translated as "kept"—*krateo*—also can be translated as "restrained," "repressed," "seized hold of," or "vanquished."

4. They look sad, but they sound. . . ?
   - What does this say about the grieving process?
5. Why does Jesus ask "What things?"
   - What does he want to know?
   - What does it do for them to tell him the things?
6. In verse 19, who do they say Jesus was?
   - How does that match up with what we have been looking at?
7. Nevertheless, they had great hopes for Israel's redemption. Does this suggest that they knew the outcome ahead of time?
8. The empty tomb was checked, but they still feel how?
9. Verses 25–27 sound like what kind of material?
10. In verse 28 they still do not recognize him, so the person they invite in is a. . . ?
11. Where did they get the idea to do something like that?
12. How does what they are doing now differ from what they were doing moments before?
13. The breaking of bread—of what is that reminiscent?
    - So again, they are doing what?
14. In verse 31, what opened their eyes?
    - Why did he vanish again?
    - If he had stayed, what might have happened?
15. In verse 35, they knew him how?
16. Following the process that moves through this passage, what does the resurrection involve within the lives of people?
    - What is the outcome in their lives?

STEP 2. Bridge-building

Ask the participants to take sheets of paper and put lines vertically down the middle. On the left side, tell them to write the parts of their lives that are dying right now. On the right side have them write the things that are rising. (This is an intentional repeat of the bridging exercise from the first sequence, Session I. The rest of the session continues as in other Session Vs.)

EPILOGUE

May your behavior rise out of your life in Jesus the Christ, who, though sharing in the divine nature of God, did not seek to play God. Rather, he cleared out his own inner space to be able to serve others. He became like other humans and shared the human condition. He stayed centered in the deepest places of himself, even as he died, even as he died on the cross. Because of this, God raised him up and has given him such an enduring identity and power that we can look to him as we learn to face all the powers that might hold us in bondage. And when we let him become active in our lives, we can let God shine through all that we do.

So, my friends, with a sense of awe and wonder, work at moving toward wholeness, for God is at work within us, mobilizing our will and transforming our behavior, helping us to move toward that for which we were created.

—*Philippians* 2:5–12a, 13
(paraphrased)

APPENDIX I

FOUR BASIC EMOTIONS

What follows is a list of the four basic emotions of joy, fear, pain, and anger, with a selection of some related words listed underneath them. In the notes, you will find references to articles that describe how these basic emotions take on special meanings in the biblical witness. These articles serve to deepen understanding of these emotions and to show how crucial they are to a fuller appreciation of the biblical witness.

Joy[1]

adequate	ecstatic	heavenly	proud
affectionate	energetic	high	refreshed
blissful	excited	honored	relaxed
bold	fascinated	infatuated	relieved
brave	free	inspired	satisfied
capable	gay	joyous	sexy
cheerful	glad	jubilant	sure
contented	good	loving	victorious
delighted	gratified	nice	wonderful
eager	happy	peaceful	zany

Fear[2]

abandoned	fearful	isolated	panicky
anxious	flustered	jumpy	petrified
astounded	frightened	nervous	restless
awed	helpless	odd	reverent
conspicuous	intimidated	overwhelmed	scared

shocked	tentative	threatened	unsettled
startled	tenuous	trapped	vulnerable
stunned	terrified	uneasy	worried
tense			

Pain[3]

abandoned	enslaved	low	solemn
agony	envious	melancholy	sorrowful
bad	exploited	miserable	starved
betrayed	foolish	offended	stupid
burdened	guilty	oppressed	suffering
cheated	homesick	overwhelmed	sympathetic
condemned	horrible	persecuted	terrible
contrite	hurt	pity	threatened
discomfort	imposed on	pressured	troubled
crushed	isolated	put down	ugly
deceitful	jealous	rejected	victimized
defeated	left out	remorse	violated
discontented	lonely	sad	weepy
enervated	longing	skeptical	

Anger[4]

adamant	cruel	incensed	rage
angry	determined	indignant	tenacious
annoyed	disturbed	infuriated	violent
bitter	exasperated	mad	vehement
bored	frustrated	mean	vengeful
combative	furious	outraged	wrath
competitive	hateful		

APPENDIX II

RAISE YOUR HOSANNAS!

How would an investigative reporter, or a detective, research the details of that big week in Jesus' life which started on "Palm Sunday"? The traditional picture that has come down to us today is of a pleasant, peaceful Jesus plodding into Jerusalem on a donkey welcomed by crowds. Yet in a seemingly very brief time he had been publicly executed by Roman soldiers.

What really happened? Of all animals to choose, why choose a donkey? What did Jesus hope to accomplish? Why did the crowds do what they did? How did people get disturbed enough about Jesus to want him out of the way? How could all that happened between "Palm Sunday" and "Good Friday" possibly have happened in those few short days?

The answers are not easy to get at. There is a lot we don't know and never will. Our main resources—the four Gospels—differ in their accounts. Even Mark, the earliest of the four (60 A.D.), was a little fuzzy about things like exactly when, where, and in what order things happened. But if you keep digging, Mark (chapter 11:1–19) provides a lot of clues which lead to some surprising answers.

The first clue is the animal. Mark says Jesus sent his

disciples for an unbroken colt *(pólôs)*. If someone sent you for a colt, what would you bring back? A horse, right? Well, that's just what the disciples probably got. The word "colt" *(pólôs)* could mean the offspring of any animal, but when used *alone* it referred to a young horse. But why an unbroken one? Because an unbroken animal was chosen when the person had a task to perform that had a special sacred significance. So already the picture is changing. There's a lot more energy and clearly Jesus was coming up to Jerusalem with a *very special purpose* in mind.

The next clue comes from the crowds who were waving green branches and shouting "Hosanna." Was there some time when they would normally be doing that? Yes, there was. In fact, there were two times—the autumn Festival of Booths, and the Feast of Dedication (Hanukkah) in December. Of the two, the Feast of Dedication is the more likely candidate for being the festival Jesus was coming up for. This needs a little explanation, especially because it was celebrated differently in Jesus' day than it is now.

The festival commemorates the cleansing of the Temple by Judas Maccabaeus and his followers in December, 165 B.C.

Three years prior to that, the Syrians had desecrated the Temple by putting an altar to Zeus on the Temple altar and by sacrificing a hog on it, which was an act of unimaginable horror to the Jews. This and other acts of subjugation of the Jewish population triggered the revolt which culminated in the cleansing of the Temple and in political independence. This oppression by the Syrians and the successful revolt under the Maccabeans were at least as significant to the Jews of Jesus' day as the events leading up to our own nation's independence are to us. This was especially true because the Jews in Jesus' day were once again under foreign domination, this time by the Romans.

The festival itself was one which drew pilgrims from all over the country to the Holy City of Jerusalem. The celebration was similar to the fall Festival of Booths or Tabernacles (II Maccabees 10:6–8). Hopes would run high for the coming of the kingdom of God, for deliverance from the foreign oppression of the Romans just as years previously the Maccabeans had overthrown the Syrians. This time, however, they felt only a miracle of God could make that happen. As the pilgrims neared Jerusalem, they would gather up leafy branches, which were called "Hosannas." As they entered Jerusalem on the way to the Temple, they would carry their "hosannas" and sing the "Hallel" (a collection of Psalms), especially Psalm 118:25–27 (RSV), which reads:

Save us
(Hosanna), we beseech thee O Lord!
O Lord, we beseech thee, give us success!
Blessed is he (the pilgrim) who comes in the name of the Lord!
We bless you from the house of the Lord.
The Lord is God and He has given us light.
Bind the festal procession with branches
Up to the horns of the altar.

At the exclamation "Hosanna," the pilgrims would wave their branches. When they got to the Temple, they would offer sacrifices of animals purchased at the Temple from sellers authorized by the Temple authorities.

If you compare this with Mark's account of Jesus' entry into Jerusalem in Chapter 11, the similarities are truly striking. I believe that Jesus intentionally chose this festival to come up to Jerusalem to carry his message to people who were supposed to have been the religious leaders of his time. The place he chose for this confrontation was their front yard, so to speak, the Temple courtyard. In order to understand the nature of the confrontation, we need to follow up on several other clues.

First, Jesus was in all likelihood thoroughly familiar

with Jerusalem and the Temple. As the son of a faithful Jewish family, he had been a frequent visitor there at festival time from childhood on. He knew the city so well by the age of 12 that his parents felt confident leaving him on his own during their stay there (Luke 2:41ff.). During his many visits to Jerusalem, he would have had ample opportunity to observe what went on at festival time, including the activities of the sellers of sacrificial animals and money-changers who did their business in the Temple precincts. These people were agents of the Temple authorities. The only animals acceptable for sacrifice were the ones sold by them and the only money you could use to buy these animals had to be purchased from them also. So there was a double monopoly, which was used to enhance the fortunes of the Temple authorities. There was a lot of resentment among the Jewish people in general about this exploitation. Jesus apparently shared this. But what he objected to just as much was the place where this trade was carried on, namely the Court of Gentiles, which was supposed to have been reserved for the non-Jewish people to worship.

This leads us then directly to the special, sacred task for which Jesus rode into Jerusalem on an unbroken animal. Just as he had called the people of the land to repentance (to change their behavior) throughout his ministry, so now he was going up to the Holy City to challenge the people who were supposed to be religious leaders—the chief priests—to challenge them to repent as well. So he went up to the Temple, drove the money-changers and animal-sellers from the Court of Gentiles, stopped people from using that area as a shortcut (11:16) and, recalling two of Israel's greatest prophets Isaiah (56:7) and Jeremiah (7:11), he challenged the Temple authorities to stop exploiting the pilgrims and to restore the Court of Gentiles to its proper use—as a place of worship "for all nations."

You'll remember that the Feast of Dedication was instituted to celebrate the cleansing of the Temple by Jews from its desecration by the Gentiles. Jesus dramatically turns this around and attempts to cleanse the Temple from its desecration by people who were supposed to have been religious *leaders*—a desecration which included shutting the Gentiles out from their rightful place in the Temple and by implication their rightful place in the promise of God (Isaiah 2:2–4).

And in the Apocryphal history of the Maccabees, you read in II Maccabees 10, where after cleansing the Temple in 165 B.C., Judas Maccabaeus prays that "the Lord not let them fall any more into such disasters (as the Syrian desecration of the Temple, etc.), but, should they ever happen to sin, to discipline them himself with clemency and not hand them over to blasphemous and barbarous Gentiles." Did Jesus then see himself as the agent of God's "discipline"?

I think he did. Much as morally sensitive Americans have been distressed to find their leaders engaging in political espionage and the like (leaders from whom they rightfully expect political *and* moral leadership), so Jesus was distressed at people not living up to the rightfully expected standards of religious and moral leadership. And he attempted to do something about that. But it was more than that.

Throughout his ministry, Jesus had reached out and included people who were written off and put down (women, children, tax collectors—even enemies!). It is fitting indeed that his last great dramatic act should be an attempt to include the Gentiles, who were at the time excluded.

If we were to take this seriously for ourselves in the present time, we'd have to ask ourselves who *we* are excluding, writing off, putting down. And then we'd have to change—allow our own "Temples" (our hearts and minds, our homes, our churches, our schools, etc.) to be cleansed and opened up. The question is whether we're willing to allow that to happen in our lives, or whether—like the chief priests of Jesus' time—we'd try to get rid of the challenge to change.

NOTES

Prologue

1. The words of John Robinson, the pastor of the Pilgrims, as they departed for the New World.

Chapter I   The Living Authority of Scripture

1. "Scribe," *Interpreter's Dictionary of the Bible* (Nashville: Abingdon Press, 1962), vol. 4, pp. 246, 248.

2. Rudolf Bultmann, *Glauben und Verstehen*, 2d ed. (Tübingen: J.C.B. Mohr [Paul Siebeck], 1954), vol. 1, pp. 126–27 (my translation).

3. Aldous Huxley, *The Doors of Perception* (New York: Harper & Row, 1954), p. 73.

4. John G. Saxe, "The Blind Men and the Elephant," *Poems* (Boston, 1852). Quoted in *Anthology of Children's Literature*, 4th rev. ed., ed. Edna Johnson, Frances Clark Sayers, Evelyn R. Sickels (Boston: Houghton Mifflin, 1970).

5. In what follows, I am indebted to Dr. Thomas Campbell both for his lecture and for a long succeeding conversation about this issue before his untimely death in 1979. As I tried to refresh my memory for this writing, I contacted Donna Campbell, and she graciously loaned me her late husband's lecture notes from the course he took from Prof. Richard McKeon, of the University of Chicago, where Campbell learned this basic scheme. As I puzzled about how to acknowledge this properly, I discovered that Prof. Donald White, of United Theological Seminary, had a mimeographed copy of Professor McKeon's lectures from which Campbell had taken notes. My thanks to Pro-

fessor White for his kindness in loaning me this copy. I want to say, however, that this presentation is my understanding and interpretation of what I learned from Thomas Campbell and has been amplified by reading. I do not claim to be presenting Professor McKeon's work as such.

6. Paul Tillich, *The Shaking of the Foundations* (New York: Charles Scribner's Sons, 1948), p. 116.

7. Ibid., p. 117.

8. John Locke, *The Reasonableness of Duty, as Delivered in the Scriptures* (1695), pp. 290–55.

9. Matthew Tindal, *Christianity as Old as the Creation of the Gospel, A Republication of the Religion of Nature* (1730), pp. 258–62.

10. Thomas Chubb, *The True Gospel of Jesus Christ, Asserted* (London, 1738), pp. 43ff., 46ff., 142.

11. Tillich, *The Shaking of the Foundations*, p. 116.

Chapter II The Style of Communication as It Affects the Authority of Scripture

1. See Sherod Miller, Elan W. Nunnelley, and David B. Wackman, *Talking Together* (Minneapolis: Interpersonal Communications Programs, 1980), for a complete presentation of this approach. Pages 103ff. deal specifically with styles of communication.

Chapter III The Dynamics of Being Human

1. Albert Schweitzer, *The Quest of the Historical Jesus* (New York: Macmillan Co., 1959).

2. For a fuller exposition, see William Miller, *Make Friends with Your Shadow* (Minneapolis: Augsburg Publishing House, 1981).

3. B. Harvie Branscomb, *The Moffatt Commentary on Mark* (New York: Harper & Bros., n.d.), p. 201.

4. Wayne B. Robinson, *Questions Are the Answer* (New York: The Pilgrim Press, 1980), pp. 51–53.

5. See Sherod Miller et al., *Talking Together* (Min-

neapolis: Interpersonal Communications Programs, 1980), pp. 25ff.

6. Walter Wink, *Transforming Bible Study* (Nashville: Abingdon Press, 1980), pp. 17–34.

7. Betty Edwards, *Drawing on the Right Side of the Brain* (Los Angeles: J. D. Tarcher, 1979).

8. Ibid., p. 35.

9. Ibid.

10. Virginia Satir, *Peoplemaking* (Palo Alto: Science and Behavior Books, 1972), p. 98.

Chapter IV   The "Moving Toward Wholeness" Method of Using Scripture

1. *Gospel Parallels*, ed. Burton H. Throckmorton Jr. (New York: Thomas Nelson & Sons, 1957).

2. Ibid., p. 10.

3. Ibid.

4. *The Collected Works of C.J. Jung* (New York: Bollingen Foundation, 1954), vol. 16, p. 47.

5. Ira Progoff, *At a Journal Workshop* (New York: Dialogue House Library, 1976).

6. See Walter Wink, *Transforming Bible Study* (Nashville: Abingdon Press, 1980), pp. 118ff.

Chapter V   First Sequence: "What Do You Want Me to Do for You?"

1. Ranier Maria Rilke, *Letters to a Young Poet*, trans. M.O. Herter Norton (New York: W.W. Norton & Co., 1962), pp. 29–30.

2. James Stephens, *Irish Fairy Tales* (New York: Macmillan Co., 1929, 1968), p. 64.

3. William James, *The Varieties of Religious Experience* (New York: Collier Books, 1961), p. 305.

4. Albert Einstein, quoted by L. Barnett, *The Universe and Dr. Einstein* (New York: Bantam Books, 1968), p. 108.

5. Elie Weisel, *Night* (New York: Hill & Wang, 1968), p. 16.

6. *Webster's Seventh New Collegiate Dictionary* (Springfield, Mass.: G. & C. Merriam Co., 1967), p. 1019.

7. *Interpreter's Dictionary of the Bible*, ed. George A. Buttrick and Keith R. Crim (Nashville: Abingdon Press, 1976).

8. Herman L. Strack and Paul Billerbeck, *Kommentar zum Neuen Testament* (Munich: C.H. Beck, 1961).

9. John Huizinga, *The Waning of the Middle Ages* (Garden City, N.Y.: Doubleday & Co., 1956), p. 10.

10. *Interpreter's Dictionary of the Bible* (1962 ed.), vol. 1, p. 256.

11. See Walter Wink, *Transforming Bible Study* (Nashville: Abingdon Press, 1980), Appendix I, pp. 155–57, for a discussion on miracles. The approach he suggests there (pp. 156–57) for miracles could be used for the temptation narrative as well.

Chapter VI   Second Sequence: "Like a Child"

1. Denise Varletta (age 11), in LISTEN TO US! © 1978 by Dorriet Kavanaugh, Workman Publishing, New York. Reprinted with permission of the publisher.

2. Richard Lewis, "Towards Beginnings," *Parabola: Myth and the Quest for Meaning* 4, no. 3 (Summer 1979): 24. Reprinted by permission.

3. C.J. Jung, "Archetypes and the Collective Unconscious," in *The Collected Works of C.J. Jung*, vol. 9-I (New York: Boliingen Foundation, 1959), p. 170.

4. Margery Williams, *The Velveteen Rabbit* (Garden City, N.Y.: Doubleday & Co., 1958), pp. 16–17.

5. From *Ministry and Imagination* by Urban T. Holmes III, pp. 187–88. Copyright © 1976 by The Seabury Press, Inc. Used by permission.

6. *Webster's Seventh New Collegiate Dictionary* (Springfield, Mass.: G. & C. Merriam Co., 1967), p. 262.

7. Herman L. Strack and Paul Billerbeck, *Kommentar*

zum Neuen Testament (Munich: C.H. Beck, 1961), vol. 1, p. 520 (my translation).

8. See the excellent article on the "Shekinah" by Dale Moody, in *Interpreter's Dictionary of the Bible*, vol. 4 (Nashville: Abingdon Press, 1962), pp. 317–19.

Chapter VII   Third Sequence: Deepening Our Spiritual Journey

1. James Stephens, *Irish Fairy Tales* (New York: Macmillan Co., 1929, 1968), p. 221.

2. John Sanford, *The Kingdom Within* (Philadelphia: J.B. Lippincott Co., 1970), p. 43.

3. Barbara C. Sproul, *Primal Myths: Creating the World* (New York: Harper & Row, 1979), p. 1.

4. Sanford, *The Kingdom Within*, p. 20.

5. Robert L. Schwenck, *Digging Deep* (Pecos, N.M.: Dove Publications, 1979), p. 12.

6. Margery Williams, *The Velveteen Rabbit* (Garden City, N.Y.: Doubleday & Co., 1958), p. 17.

7. See Norman Perrin, *Rediscovering the Teaching of Jesus* (New York: Harper & Row, 1967), pp. 69ff.

8. Ibid., p. 74.

9. See Wayne B. Robinson, *Questions Are the Answer* (New York: The Pilgrim Press, 1980), pp. 15–16.

10. Barry Holstun Lopez, *River Notes* (Kansas City, Kans.: Andrews & McNeel, 1979), pp. 74–75.

11. Quoted in *Gospel Parallels*, ed. Burton H. Throckmorton Jr. (New York: Thomas Nelson & Sons, 1957), p. 11.

12. This way of using one's childlike imagination is beautifully described in Richard de Mille's *Put Your Mother on the Ceiling* (New York: Walker & Co., 1967). It also contains some delightful imagination exercises.

13. *Environments, Disc 8*, Side 2: *A Country Stream*, Syntomic Research, 175 Fifth Avenue, New York, N.Y.

10010. For a description of the Jabbok River, see *Interpreter's Dictionary of the Bible*, vol. 2 (Nashville: Abingdon Press, 1962), p. 778. (The Jabbok name may have come from its gurgling sound.)

14. Perrin, *Rediscovering the Teaching of Jesus* (New York: Harper & Row, 1967), pp. 54–108.

15. Robinson, *Questions Are the Answer*, pp. 65–72.

16. Sanford, *The Kingdom Within*.

Chapter VIII Fourth Sequence: Getting at the Christian Story Inside Us

1. Günther Bornkamm, *Jesus of Nazareth* (New York: Harper & Bros., 1960), p. 55.

2. Joachim Jeremias, *Jerusalem in the Time of Jesus* (Philadelphia: Fortress Press, 1977).

3. Ibid., p. 25.

4. Ibid., pp. 32ff.

5. See *Interpreter's Dictionary of the Bible*, vol. 1 (Nashville: Abingdon Press, 1962), pp. 748–49.

Appendix I Four Basic Emotions

1. See "Joy," in *Interpreter's Dictionary of the Bible*, vol. 2 (Nashville: Abingdon Press, 1962), pp. 1000–1001; "*Chairo*," etc., in *Theological Dictionary of the New Testament*, ed. Gerhard Kittel and Gerhard Friedrich, trans. Geoffrey W. Bromiley (Grand Rapids: Wm. B. Eerdmans Publishing Co., 1974), vol. 9, pp. 359–415.

2. See "Fear," in *Interpreter's Dictionary of the Bible* vol. 2, pp. 256–60; "*Phóbos*," in *Theological Dictionary of the New Testament*, vol. 9, pp. 189–219.

3. See "Mourning," in *Interpreter's Dictionary of the Bible*, vol. 3, pp. 452–54; "Sorrow," in ibid., vol. 4, p. 427; "Suffering and Evil," in ibid., vol. 4, pp. 450–53; "*Lúpā*," in *Theological Dictionary of the New Testament*, vol. 4, pp. 313–22.

4. See "Anger," in *Interpreter's Dictionary of the Bible*, vol. 1, pp. 135–37; "*Thumós*," in *Theological Dictionary of the New Testament*, vol. 3, pp. 167–68; "*Orgā*," in ibid., vol. 5, pp. 383–447.